D1020043

THE
Nixon Watch

Osborn

THE
Nixon Watch

BY

JOHN OSBORNE

Illustrated by ROBERT OSBORN

Introduction by TOM WICKER

LIVERIGHT

NEW YORK

1.987654321

This book consists of articles that appeared in *The New Republic* between October 1968 and January 1970. Its title, *The Nixon Watch,* is the standing head under which John Osborne reports the Nixon Presidency for that magazine. Apart from some changes of tense for present clarity, the correction of typographical and similar errors, and the addition of updating addenda at the end of a few chapters, the originals have not been altered for this publication. All articles are reprinted by permission of the publisher.

Standard Book Number: 87140–502–4
Library of Congress
Catalog Card Number: 76–114384
DESIGNED BY VINCENT TORRE
Manufactured in the United States of America

CONTENTS

INTRODUCTION

BY TOM WICKER

Even after a year of power, the Nixon Administration appeared to fit none of those figurative pigeonholes over which the familiar labels of American politics have been so carefully taped. It wasn't "liberal," but was it "conservative" in the usual sense? Not even the big pigeonhole in the middle marked "moderate" permitted a good fit. Some say that even "Republican" won't quite do.

The point at which to begin describing this Administration is negative; it is clearly *not* just the Eisenhower Administration, eight years removed. This is not a government of Wall Street lawyers (save those of Mr. Nixon's old firm), Boston Brahmins, the major corporations, the Ivy League college presidents, or the New York Council on Foreign Relations. The Mormon former president of a Chicago bank presides at the House of Mellon, the Cabinet boasts Italian Catholic and Southern Protestant construction men, a frontier entrepreneur from Alaska, one of Detroit's hottest auto salesmen, a shorthaired California politician, and a Secretary of Defense out of the plebian House of Representatives by way of the lumber industry. Mr. Nixon at the White House is surrounded by West Coast advertising executives and young merchandising types, and in perhaps the most spectacular single act of his Administration, a Republican Vice President of Greek-American lineage actually attacked the Eastern Establishment, or at least the press and television he said were the Establishment's creatures. That loud whirring noise was bound to have been from the graves of Nicholas Murray Butler, the elder Lodge, and Joe Pew.

Mr. Nixon, it is obvious, eulogizes Ike, honors Mamie, and displays David; but when it comes to politics and government, the Administration he has put together is a new breed of cat. No doubt partially based also on his own rank-and-file origins, nondescript college, and relentless perception of Americans as mostly middle-class, God-fearing football fans, Mr. Nixon's government is primarily a product of the times, which are a-changin'.

Its most identifiable and controversial bloodline derives from the famous Forgotten American of the Nixon Campaign, who now lives somewhere amid the Great Silent Majority. The Forgotten American knows no North or South, no West and less East, nor as much party as he used to. Typically, he seems to have fled the approach of the ghetto and the isolation of the country to establish himself in the suburbs and the small towns. He worries about crime, immorality, unrest, prices, and taxes. He would not be caught dead rioting or demonstrating, and suspects most of those who do are either duped by foreign agents or irresponsible. He is not "against" blacks but thinks they are getting too much, too fast, for too little effort, and he can prove that their presence in the neighborhood lowers hard-earned values and in the schools destroys long-established standards. He fears that welfare damages character and costs too much, thinks that a hardline police policy would deter crime and violence, and believes that his own children do not play around with pot, drugs, the Students for a Democratic Society, or pre-marital sex. He is fed up with a war that is not being won, but shocked at the notion of an American defeat. And he is inclined to agree with J. Edgar Hoover that justice is only incidental to the maintenance of order.

The Forgotten American of today is, in fact, the old traditional salt of the earth frustrated by and in reaction against years of up-rooting population growth and migration at home, and a quarter-century of unrewarding political and military management abroad—against burgeoning affluence, exploding technology, declining individualism; but the targets of his reaction are not so much these ill-understood forces themselves as the standards and institutions that have been outmoded and overwhelmed by them—first of all, the government itself and the New Deal liberal philosophy that has made it so big and so expensive for the better part of 40 years.

If this description of the Forgotten American seems derogatory, it is nonetheless one which emerges from much of the rhetoric and programming of the Nixon Administration. The Justice Department's punitive approach to crime and civil disorder, as exemplified in its so-called "preventive detention" proposals as well as in the claim that black militant and student groups can be secretly but legally wiretapped as threats to the national security; the attempted slowdown in the pace of Southern school desegregation and the undercutting of the Johnson Administration's effective Voting Rights Act for Southern blacks; the nomination of conservative jurists to what used to be the Warren Court; the persistent talk of modifying that court's decisions asserting the rights of defendants; the use of a conspiracy statute to prosecute those who allegedly plotted the 1968 violence in Chicago; the hortatory appeals to patriotism, national pride, and anti-Communist instincts, as a counter to the anti-Vietnam war movement; the studied rebuff to and downgrading of the October and November 1969 protest demonstrations—all of these are of a parcel. They represented not just a limited "Southern Strategy" designed only to counter George Wallace and win votes in Dixie, although that purpose may be served; not merely a supine surrender to minor potentates like Strom Thurmond and John Tower; but rather the genuine political response, no less considered for being at times instinctive, of an Administration that believes the Forgotten American constitutes a Great Silent Majority, hence rightfully must be served—an Administration also that in important respects appears to share, hence respect, the Forgotten American's view of and reaction to society and the times.

After a year of Nixonian government, there is not much doubt that it is most strongly influenced by the idea that the Forgotten American is the dominant political figure of the day—that not much can be done without his support, and even less against his active opposition. This is not to suggest that no other intellectual, political and spiritual forces were at work within this Administration; if it had been engaged in nothing other than a sympathetic head-shrinking of the Great Silent Majority, it would neither be hard to classify nor worth much study. The point is, rather, that other strong influences—of which there appeared to be at least two—made themselves felt but not without important reference to the Forgotten-Man theology that lies at the heart of the Administration.

Another powerful impulse, basically domestic, is not—for instance—so much revisionist, not so much bemused by longing for a simpler and more manageable order of things at home and abroad, as the Forgotten American is widely supposed to be; instead, it springs from the conviction that the urban liberals who have dominated government since Franklin Roosevelt have muffed the job. Those who feel this way see, for instance, four major civil rights bills in a decade but a worse racial crisis than ever; federal aid to an education system that doesn't work, at least not well enough; a "war on poverty" that not only ended in defeat but virtually discredited the effort; a massive attack on urban ills that has left the cities in even greater disarray and tension; a welfare program that creates more dependency, rather than relieving it; and a vast federal bureaucracy, allied to a Democratic Congress, that scatters available dollars and energies more nearly according to political power relationships and long-established criteria than in pursuit of realistic goals and responsible priorities.

If Attorney General John Mitchell is the symbol of the influence of the Forgotten Man, Daniel Patrick Moynihan, the President's Democratic urban counsellor, has probably been the most articulate representative of those whose primary impulse is to make government work, to better match its performance to its promise.

It was not too difficult for those who follow Mitchell and those who take Moynihan's view to make common cause. In the first place, the Forgotten American generally doesn't think government has been working either, if for a differing complex of reasons; thus there was a common political base to be built upon by men who also shared a disillusionment with the liberal dogmas of past decades, and with the liberal political and bureaucratic establishment that produced and conformed to them.

Out of somewhat differing motivations, therefore, come roughly common aims—for instance, that the number of persons dependent on welfare should be reduced—and, in pursuit of these aims, each can make allowances for the other. Moynihan may have had to tolerate Mitchell's attack on the voting rights bill in order to pursue his plans on welfare, but those plans may win a greater acceptance than would have been possible in an Administration committed to the established liberal concepts and apprehensions.

So the most significant result of this second strain of influence within the Nixon Administration seemed to be its adoption—not yet followed by Congressional approval—of the outlines of an "income approach" to the welfare-poverty problem. While the complex Family Assistance Plan falls considerably short of what is generally meant by "guaranteed annual income," it takes three long steps in that direction. It establishes the notion of a "right" to income; it would therefore deliver assistance in the form of cash and food stamps rather than in services; and it makes the "working poor" as well as the indigent eligible for help.

The Family Assistance Plan has many flaws, primarily the low income at first to be provided, and faces hard going in a Democratic Congress; it constitutes, nevertheless, the most substantial welfare reform proposal in the program's history. It is remarkable for today's climate in that it actually would put more people on the rolls and cost the taxpayers more money than the existing version. In the long run, it is calculated to reduce dependency through income incentives and work-training; but probably only an Administration that commands the confidence of the Forgotten Americans could hope to win public support for it against its short-run liabilities.

Another rather fluid product of the make-government-work influence is the Administration's revenue-sharing proposals. These, too, are a long way from Congressional approval, and at the proposed funding level would not at first have great impact anyway. Continuing Democratic and liberal influence in the cities, as against the widespread Republican dominance of statehouses, gives the states first place in the receiving line for the federal funds to be shared, although the states are supposed to let a proportionate share trickle down to the cities. Since cities like New York can demonstrate greater need for money than many states, but since the cities need it mainly for programs that may arouse the animosity of the Forgotten Man, trouble is brewing on this vital point.

Whatever its drawbacks, revenue-sharing is another effort to get the kind of results from federal funds that many believe the big federal agencies, matching-grant programs, with their uniform criteria, inflexible administration and bureaucratic concerns, have not been able to produce. And the plan has another theoretical advantage: if successful, it would place operational responsibility for social programs in state and local jurisdictions, which might tend both to rejuvenate these levels of government and give citizens a more direct voice in their affairs. Here again, in short, is something that may prove a useful reform, yet ought to sound sensible to the Forgotten American; and so it becomes palatable in the Nixon Administration.

Similarly, if government is going to be made to work, one of the things it will have to do is to spend its money where it most needs spending. This has been brought home sharply to men like Moynihan by their developing conviction that the liberal faith of the sixties—the nation can afford anything it really wants to do, feeding the poor as well as fighting the Communist—was misplaced, that the play of domestic and international political forces on the national wealth places a finite limit on funds that will be available for social programs. It was Moynihan the liberal, not a Pentagon general, who publicly disputed the idea of a sizeable "peace dividend" following the end of the war in Vietnam. Here again is an attitude that can make something of a common cause with those who wish to appease the Forgotten Man; and indeed it has been the Nixon Administration that has managed a significant reduction in the Pentagon's budget, everybody's favorite target for misplaced federal money.

A third strain of significant opinion within Mr. Nixon's house appears, again, to duplicate strong public sentiment. It holds that while there is no responsible way to abandon the world role thrust upon the nation in World War II and after, the manner in which recent Administrations have played that role has been too militant and too military, therefore too dangerous and too expensive, and that what is needed in the 1970s—both in the cause of world stability and American domestic welfare—is "lower profile" in foreign policy and a resolute rejection of the notion of playing policeman in a world where, anyway, the old notion of monolithic Communism on the march no longer seems to apply.

Thus, Mr. Nixon's repeated slogan about an era of confrontation giving way to an era of negotiation. Thus, the SALT talks. Thus, "Vietnamization" of the war. Thus, the Nixon Doctrine for Asia, and the reopening of talks with China. And without this attitude, the military spending reductions could not realistically have been attained.

Here, however, the Forgotten Man becomes a more troublesome supporter. The Johnson Administration seemed ready to move considerably further than Mr. Nixon had on nuclear arms talks as of the beginning of the new decade. Vietnamization is, at best, a long, slow process, costly in lives and money—and, at worst, a formula for maintaining a proxy war for no one knows how many years. The Nixon Doctrine sounded, as Vice President Agnew described it in Asia, like six of Nixon and a half-dozen of Johnson. The Chinese talks owed as much to Peking's fear of Moscow as to Mr. Nixon's liberalism. And while the Pentagon budget has been cut, the Administration is going ahead with ABM and MIRV.

The limited nature of all these moves, while congenial to the world view Mr. Nixon has always expressed, nevertheless suggests a profound respect for the powerful impulses, prejudices, and convictions of all those Forgotten Men—who are supposed to believe in the might as well as the right of America, the iniquity of the Russians and the Communist Chinese, and the necessity of standing as tough in the world as Marshall Dillon or the Kansas City Chiefs.

This in its turn suggests the basic limitation of an Administration determined to establish a kind of linkage between its own aims and ideals and those of what it believes to be the controlling political sentiment of the country. It is likely to hold itself to what can be justified politically—in a phrase John Erlichman once used, to an act that will "play in Peoria." It is likely to calculate its program more on the basis of what it believes the dominant forces want than on what ought to be done in some broader concept of the public good and need. It may sacrifice the role of leader and teacher in order to maintain political standing. Worse, in its effort to divine a national mood, it may badly underestimate—or allow its own beliefs to influence its realistic judgment of—what the people can be persuaded to support. Did Mr. Nixon underestimate, for example, the extent to which Americans generally would support a negotiated peace that did not sustain the Thieu-Ky government in South Vietnam?

On the other hand, it can well be argued that the people had had quite enough of Roosevelt-Kennedy-Johnson style "leadership" toward goals that were not commonly accepted or understood and that this high-powered approach to government produced too few results, solved too few problems, and roused too many animosities, however exciting it was. It can also be argued, for instance, that if in a democracy the majority of the people think blacks are getting too much, too fast, that belief is the salient fact that has to be reckoned with; so it makes sense to build toward a policy that will convince the white majority no one segment of the population is being favored to the disadvantage of another. Only then, as this line of argument runs, can an Administration successfully put through such an innovative step as the "Philadelphia Plan" to increase the number of blacks employed in the construction trades.

All that can be argued, and has been. The case can be made, even more strongly, that it is dangerous for government to arouse among blacks, or the poor generally, or any other groups, expectations that it cannot fulfill because it does not have the money or the knowledge or the political support, or all three. In sum, it is certainly better for the government to work than for it not to work, and it is all too true that it has not worked well enough in the past.

There remains a real danger for a government based too strongly upon identification with a majority united primarily in bitterness, mistrust, fear, and anger. And this is a point that was not lost on John Osborne as he kept watch on Nixon week by week for *The New Republic* throughout the first year. The danger is that those who seek the favor and support of such a majority may encourage, and themselves emulate, these qualities, rather than trying to build, too, upon those other strains of generosity and courage that many a President has found not lacking in the American people.

If the Nixon Administration defies classification, after all, how much more do the times and "the people"! Not just the Forgotten Man—himself a none too well-known quantity, a flesh-and-blood human rather than a poll-taker's cipher—but the blacks, the students, the liberals of Park Avenue, the *Chicanos,* the intellectuals, the businessmen, the affluent suburbanites, the welfare recipients, the old, the young, the Appalachian poor—all the infinite variety of a continental democracy in ferment and turmoil, caught in the explosive change of the twentieth century. It would be a curious political view that saw some static majority, fixed and definable, dominating all these other forces even for one Presidential term, let alone a new political era; and surely an Administration that understood and concerned itself only with a part of the seething whole, no matter how large that part, would not be asking the best of itself or of the nation.

THE
Nixon Watch

The Candidate Nixon

At the Nixon rally in Minneapolis on the night of October 8, I sat in the press section between Joseph Alsop and Mrs. Sandy Fendrick of Hutchinson, Minnesota, who heads the Women's Committee for Nixon-Agnew in McLeod County. She is a pretty woman in her thirties, and that night she was aglow with pride in her candidate, Richard Nixon, and in the work that she and her friends in McLeod had done for him. Never in Hutchinson and in the county, she said, had so many people of all ages and parties worked so hard for a candidate, and she had with her an impressive list of committees and names and activities to prove it. Two buses had been hired at $45 each and filled with over 100 Nixon rooters, about half of them youngsters of college and high school age, for the 40-mile trip from Hutchinson to Minneapolis. Scores of other buses from other towns were lined outside the hall, and all of them had brought contingents of young Minnesotans who were now assembled on the main floor and in the gallery levels just above it, chanting and clapping and stomping on cue for Nixon. Although they and Mrs. Fendrick could not have known it, their measured and clearly commanded responses gave this occasion, with its crowd of 8,000 Minnesotans, the same air of contrived and managed enthusiasm that, in city after city, had made me and other reporters traveling with the Nixon party wonder whether we, no less than the people in the crowds, were participants in a monstrous illusion of acclaim and pending victory for Richard Nixon. I was listening with half an ear to Mr. Nixon, enacting his standard rally performance with the same gestures, the same words, the same elided promises of a new leadership— seeming to promise without finally promising more security, more "peace at home and peace abroad" for less money at less risk— that he delivers everywhere; and listening also to Mrs. Fendrick, who was saying between cheers that the man performing for her was all that she had thought he was and wanted him to be, when Joe Alsop rasped out one of the amiable savageries for which he is famous among his acquaintances. "He reminds me of a trained chimpanzee," Alsop growled, glaring up at Mr. Nixon. "I keep waiting for him to scratch himself."

Like other wearers of the Nixon press badge, pampered and cosseted and served as no campaign reporters have ever been before, I keep waiting for Mr. Nixon to show himself. At this writing, in the fourth week of travel just behind him (not really "with him," as we like to think), I know that I and my companions wait in vain. Richard Milhous Nixon, the Nixon who is certain now that he will be the next President of the United States, is not going to show himself to us and to the electorate in any way that will tell us anywhere near as much as we need to know and are entitled to know about him and the Presidency that he proposes to give us. I have written that Mr. Nixon is asking the Americans whose votes he does not hope to get, the Americans who are not naturally drawn to him and into his centrist coalition of frustration, to take him on faith and await his proof, in office and action, that he will be a more liberal and humane and creative President than he promises to be. It is clear now, less than three weeks before voting day, that Mr. Nixon is not only asking but requiring all Americans, including the affluent and unhappy and

Osborn

fearful "forgotten Americans" to whom he appeals most forth-rightly, to take him on faith that he will be the kind of President that they in their myriad differences have been led to think he will be.

We of the accompanying press, who flatter ourselves with the notion that we never grant to any candidate the degree of faith he demands, debate with boring and incessant fervor the question that Mr. Nixon himself posed to a bunch of high school students the other day. "Is there a new Nixon?" he asked, thanking them with a smile for being too polite to raise the question. "All I can say is this, you've got to look at the man, you've got to answer the question yourself." It was a typical Nixon moment—loaded with frankness, with a readiness to call up and laugh at his con-troversial past, and totally lacking in clues to the answer that, he tells the American electorate, we have to find for ourselves. After looking at him and listening to him for the better part of a month, the only answer I have to offer is that it is a silly question. There is *a* Nixon, *this* Nixon, the Nixon who is telling me and

all Americans that he is going to defeat Hubert Humphrey and
George Wallace on November 5 and be our next President, and
I am damned if I know who the man is and what kind of Presi-
dent he is likely to be.

If there is in the foregoing a note of complaint that Mr. Nixon
is not telling and showing me what I ought to be able to discover
for myself, it is not accidental and it is not unique with me. Mr.
Nixon knows about the complaint, knows why it exists, and he
gets a kick out of fomenting it. "It's a lot of fun and I don't mind
it," he told a television interviewer in Dallas, in the course of
deriding the "many people" who are reduced to trying to "psycho-
analyze what I happen to be at this time." He congratulates himself in public upon the belief that his "handling of the press" is
more "effective" in this campaign than it was in 1960. So it is:
he and his assistants handle us very well indeed, so well that we
as a group supinely submit to evasions and phony spokesmanship
by underlings and a show of distant warmth that ought to be,
but somehow are not, more offensive than the cold contempt
with which he generally treated the 1960 press corps. Judging
from what his staff tells me about him, however, I doubt that
Mr. Nixon is accurately informed about and comprehends the
predominant feeling toward him among the reporters who follow
him across the country. It seems to me that we as a group—here
I speak about and not for my companions—share a sense that
Richard Nixon ought to be faulted for a fundamental lack of
political honor, for what he is doing to the political process with
his tactics of concealment and pseudo-disclosure of himself, and
resent our inability to establish a just and factual basis for
saying so.
    This is a way of saying that Mr. Nixon is very, very good at
his job, which is winning the Presidency, and that the accompanying press is not nearly so good at its job, which is to document his capacity or incapacity to be President. The reporters
who undertake only to report what the man says and what the
man does in public may question so broad a definition of their
job, but most of them act as if they had or would like to have
a larger responsibility. They, like the big-name commentators

and correspondents who join the Nixon tour for two or three days, then dart off to Humphrey and maybe Wallace, and then back to Nixon, demand their 10 or 15 minutes in private with the candidate and, denied that much, at least a ride on "Nixon One"—the *Tricia* named for his older daughter—where there is always a chance that the candidate will leave his forward cabin and mingle for a few minutes with the reporters traveling aft. Most of the writing reporters travel on the second of three United Airlines 727s, the *Julie* (for his second daughter), and the electronic fellows with their tons of gear follow on the *David* (for Julie's fiancé, General Eisenhower's grandson). Our employers, it should be noted, pay first-class fares for the jet transport, but the remaining cost to the Nixon campaign for the extra services, the abundant food and the unlimited liquor, not to mention the amenities provided at every stop of any length, must be staggering. It is reasonable to suppose that Mr. Nixon has the munificence of his campaign operation in mind when he says, as he did in a television interview with Mike Wallace of CBS, that, "Believe me, when you've gone through the fires of having to work your way through school, of having to fight campaigns with no money, of having to do it all on your own, you come out a pretty strong man and you're not in awe of anybody."

It is a rare interviewer, whether on camera or with pencil and paper, who draws that kind of remark from Richard Nixon. The reporters who wangle a session with him, and the many others who badger the members of his staff for some inkling of that hidden figure, "the real Nixon," usually confess in private and sometimes in writing that they have learned little or nothing about *him*. They may be impressed—they almost always are—with the now famous and amply lauded "Nixon operation" and with the staff, including senior members of his New York law firm, which conducts the operation. A result and, I suspect, the calculated result, is a tendency to let the operation obscure the candidate. One of the in-and-out observers, a correspondent known for his acute insights, remarked after extensive sessions with the Nixon staff that he was greatly impressed by what he had heard but was still as "mystified and confused" by it all as he had previously been. Yes, I said, so was everybody in the vicinity; but what did he think, after his labors, about Mr. Nixon? "Well," the correspondent said after a prolonged pause for thought, "I think that Mr. Nixon certainly knows how to run a campaign."

Mr. Nixon and his spokesmen encourage the assumption that a candidate who knows how to run a campaign must know how to run the country—just as, it also is said, a Republican party that can unify itself behind Mr. Nixon must know how to unify the country under his leadership. Granting that the conduct of a presidential campaign provides some clues to the candidate's conduct in the Presidency, what do we see in candidate Nixon? We see a man who manages himself extremely well and conducts himself with great skill in situations which he controls, but does not do so well in situations which he cannot wholly control. Compared with Vice President Humphrey, for instance, Mr. Nixon has been subjected to very little heckling at his rallies and other public meetings. But the little he has encountered has invariably thrown him off stride. His normally resonant voice becomes hoarse and strained, he cuts his speeches short, and he is not nearly so happy as he pretends to be when the cheering sections in his audiences—"The Nixon people," he calls them—have to roar down the hecklers. The Nixon operation, in fact, consists in large part of placing Mr. Nixon only in situations which he can expect to control. He has said that he welcomes "the tough questions" and detests the "patsies" thrown at him at press conferences. Maybe so; but he holds very few press conferences, obviously dislikes and tries to avoid follow-up questions aimed at puncturing his stock answers, and has granted interviews for quotation only to television stations along his route. In these he does impressively well, knowing as he must that what he says will be transmitted as he says it, and will—given his skill at overriding the sharpest of on-camera interviewers—leave with his audiences the impressions that he chooses to leave. His rally audiences are organized by his staff and used by him essentially as if they were vast studio audiences, with the regretted difference that they are liable to occasional though minor disruption. His most highly favored form of public address is the paid telecast, with a panel nominated by local Republican leaders and finally cleared by Nixon staffers. The questioners are free to ask whatever comes

to mind, without explicit advance notice to Mr. Nixon, but his answers make it clear that he has detailed knowledge of each panelist's background and views and knows in general what to expect from them.

Mr. Nixon has told us to expect from him a strong Presidency and a strong leadership, a Presidency conducted and a leadership exercised in a way that "will command the respect of the American people." The important thing to him in that office, he has said, would not be whether he is loved by the people or disliked by the people, but whether he is respected. In withholding so much of himself during the campaign, in displaying a public personality so cautious, so carefully molded for appearance and effect, he does convey an impression not of Joe Alsop's chimpanzee but of a kind of political automaton. He is, one gathers, husbanding his inner self and his real abilities, "the real Nixon," for a supreme effort to earn in the office he seeks the respect of which he speaks. It looks now as if he will be called upon to make the effort, and that we have no choice but to await it and whatever it tells us about Richard Nixon.

The Beginning

Three times in the first week of the Nixon Presidency, on successive afternoons, a White House electrician led the Nixon dogs, a French poodle named Vickie and a tiny Yorkshire terrier named Pasha, through the lobby where reporters and photographers assigned to the White House wait for something to happen. On Monday, while President Nixon was watching his Inaugural parade, the dogs were whisked through the lobby at a fast trot, pulling back on their leashes and evidently resenting the pace. Their keeper let them pause long enough on Tuesday for a White House usher to say to them, "Just don't decorate the floor," and for their presence to register with the photographers. The cameramen bestirred themselves on Wednesday, some cute pictures appeared in the next day's newspapers and, their mission accomplished, Vickie and Pasha were not seen again in the press lobby.

One of the first announcements from the Nixon press office was that the new Cabinet (minus Interior Secretary Walter J. Hickel, who had still to be confirmed) would assemble in the East Room of the White House at 7:30 a.m. on Wednesday and be sworn in by Chief Justice Warren at 8 a.m. Why at that in-

human hour? Because, the official answer went, "the President is anxious to meet with his Cabinet early in the morning, at 8 a.m." NBC's "Today" show is on the air at that hour. The timing won for President Nixon 25 minutes of national television coverage of an event that he could expect to dominate and did.

The first Nixon week was like that all the way—well managed, staged to get the effects and convey the impression that President Nixon wanted to get and convey. It was a good week for him, a good start for the 37th Presidency, and in that sense a good week for the country. He showed his satisfaction with it, the confidence it gave him, by exposing himself at the start of his second week to the trial of a televised press conference, which he had been expected to avoid for a while. The impression he conveyed was that of a modest man, a prosaic and ordinary man, everybody's man, early to work and not imprudently late to bed, at ease in the Presidency and, from the hour of his Inaugural, in firm command of the office and the country.

In command, that is, in the subdued Nixon style. His first public act on his first working day was to call the press to his office in the Oval Room of the West Wing and, in his matter-of-fact way, direct attention to the changes he had already made. Lyndon Johnson's big desk was gone and in its place was a smaller desk of dark, reddish wood that President Woodrow Wilson had first placed in the room and that he, Mr. Nixon, had used at the Capitol when he was General Eisenhower's Vice President. "It's a very simple desk, I like its simplicity," President Nixon said. "As you notice," he also said, "I moved out the TV set and the wires." The "TV set" had been the bank of three sets, each tuned to a major network, that along with muffled AP and UPI tickers had served Mr. Johnson's passion for instant and total access to the news. Mr. Nixon probably did not know just how much of his predecessor's ways and character he had banished. With its elaborate remote controls, the TV installation had cost $13,000. Because Mr. Johnson could not abide waiting for the sets to warm up, the picture tubes were turned on all day and all night, silent and unseen behind the electrically controlled doors of the console except when he pressed (or "mashed," in his word) appropriate buttons at his desk and the doors opened and the sound came up on the channel he wanted to hear. Gone, too,

though Mr. Nixon did not draw attention to the fact, were the two official photographers who in Mr. Johnson's time had taken at least 250,000 pictures of him at work, with his associates, with his family and grandchildren, for the mammoth personal record to be preserved at the Johnson Library in Texas. Mr. Nixon's staff photographer ("Ollie" Atkins, late of the late *Saturday Evening Post*) is under orders to snap him only on formal occasions, for a public rather than a personal record.

It was for small signs of change, rather than for the staged events and the big announcements, that the week would be remembered. One of the changes was in the Nixon smile. The appalling, on-order smile that had been seen so often during the campaign, the upward twitch followed on the instant by a return to the usual sullen set of the mouth, had been replaced, at least for the week of accession, by a slower and steadier smile. It was a believable smile, one that Mr. Nixon could hold for seconds, and it was a great improvement.

Another small and extraordinary event occurred at a reception, also on the first working Tuesday, for some 1,300 campaign workers in the East Room. President Nixon invited Mrs. Nixon to speak in his presence on a public occasion. Usually, when Patricia Nixon is with her husband in public, she appears to have withdrawn into some remote and silent world of her own—with eyes closed or, if they are open, staring out from her gaunt face at what only she may see. Painfully often during the election campaign, and at one at least of the six Inaugural balls, Mr. Nixon failed to introduce his wife. Now, at the White House reception, he did with "Here is Pat," and she uttered 53 words. Some of them were that "instead of having the 'big-shots,' so-called, we are going to have all our friends on a rotation basis. We hope to see you here again soon." Mr. Nixon, ever the vigilant guardian of himself, said as his wife turned away, "Just to keep the record clear, all of our friends are 'big shots.' " Her press secretary and Mr. Nixon's press secretary frequently told reporters during the remainder of the week that the Nixons dined together on five straight nights and on one night at midweek toured the White House together. On this tour, a spokesman acknowledged, Mrs. Nixon got her first look at Mr. Nixon's office in the Oval Room, which is perhaps a minute's walk from the adjoining Mansion.

At his first meeting with the press in the Oval Room, Mr. Nixon casually remarked that he was going to set a precedent by using a second office in the old and capacious Executive Office Building, across West Executive Avenue from the White House proper and its West Wing. "I like to work in a relatively small room with my papers all around," Mr. Nixon explained. "When I have to do brain work, I'll go over there." Also, he said, he would be closer there to his speech writers and to most of the National Security Council staff. The only offices in the old-fashioned EOB that the President would conceivably use are bigger than his Oval Room office, the one picked for him is much bigger, and he would actually be farther from rather than nearer his key NSC people. A Presidential office in the EOB would, however, have one effect and possibly another that Mr. Nixon did not mention. It would diminish the burning yen of every Presidential staffer to be quartered near him in the West Wing, where there is space only for the favored few and less space than ever for them now that Vice President Spiro T. Agnew is, by Mr. Nixon's order, also ensconced there. And a Nixon office across the way might in time reconcile the White House reporters and

cameramen to being accommodated over there, too, thus freeing
the West Wing and the President of their demanding and obtru-
sive presence. Mr. Nixon and some of his advisers had considered forcing the move upon the press and had been dissuaded
from it with considerable difficulty by Herbert Klein, the President's long-time spokesman and his new Director of Communications for the entire Executive Branch. A suspicion that the journalists accredited to the White House may yet be expelled from their
cherished haven near the President was the only curdling element
in Mr. Nixon's otherwise cozy relationship with the press during
his first week. A related suspicion that the President, working
through the quiet and clever Mr. Klein, intends to do what he
can to control and "coordinate" the flow of news about his Administration, for its advantage, would not quiet down, either,
despite the earnest efforts of Messrs. Klein and Ronald Ziegler,
the former adman who is Mr. Nixon's press secretary, to convince the skeptics that nothing is more distant from the Nixon
mind. Mr. Nixon's and their aim, they said again and again, is
"a fully open Administration." In the past, he has been anything
but an "open" man. Now the word at the Nixon White House
is that his past is done with, that it should not be read as prologue
to the Nixon Presidency.

———

The press was removed in early 1970 from the West Lobby to
larger quarters, still in the West Wing but out of the line of
passage to and from the President's office.

III

A Pass
for Mitchell

Senator James O. Eastland of Mississippi, chairman of the Senate Judiciary Committee, spoke as follows to Attorney General-designate John N. Mitchell at the start of the committee hearing on the Mitchell nomination: "I think I know your background. I think you will make a very fine Attorney General. I'm going to vote to confirm you. I have no questions."

Mr. Mitchell, a solemn and jowly man of 55, murmured his thanks and nodded as if the Senator's incuriosity were perfectly natural. In a way, it was. That part of the nominee's background that most concerned Senator Eastland was well and sufficiently known to the committee. It was of such a nature and so well-known to the committee's only Southern Republican member, Strom Thurmond of South Carolina, that he stayed away from the public portion of the hearing. He appeared only at the closed session which followed, in time to vote with all of the others

present to approve the nomination and have it ready, along with those of other Cabinet appointees, for confirmation by the Senate immediately after the Inauguration of the new President. Senator Thurmond presumably intended his absence from the public hearing to be what it was, a favor to Mr. Mitchell. Their collaboration at and after the Republican convention in August, in the interest of convincing Southern delegates and white Southern voters that Richard Nixon took a sympathetic view of their problems with racial integration and kindred matters, had achieved its purposes with his nomination and election and had become an embarrassment. The memory of it had contributed materially to the impression, by no means confined to Southerners, that Attorney General Mitchell would be inclined to enforce civil rights with a maximum of restraint and generally to influence the Nixon Administration toward a minimal use of federal power and resources for social ends.

Some of the questions put to Mr. Mitchell at the hearing reflected these apprehensions and some of his cool answers could, if closely and critically analyzed, be interpreted to support them. But the sharpest of the questions were not very sharp, others that cried for asking were not asked at all, and—the anticipated vote of approval aside—the occasion proved to be a substantial plus for Mr. Mitchell.

It was set up to be a plus. Chairman Eastland had no sooner concluded his brief accolade than New York's liberal Republican, Senator Jacob Javits, slid into the witness chair beside Mr. Mitchell and, with "very special pride," vouched for the nominee as "one of our most outstanding lawyers in New York." Neither Mr. Javits, the only witness other than Mr. Mitchell, nor any Senator on the committee mentioned the nominee's rather narrow field of legal expertise, which consists of telling local and state governments how to qualify their bond issues for public sale. Senator Sam Ervin of North Carolina, a passionate Southern constitutionalist and, when he chooses to be, a relentless pettifogger, wanted only to know whether Mr. Mitchell, a Nixon law partner who managed the Nixon campaign, intends as Attorney General

to be a political as well as a legal adviser to President Nixon. A legal adviser only, Mitchell said without a discernible tremor. Senator John McClellan of Arkansas also had a single question— whether Attorney General Mitchell proposes to use the power voted by Congress last year (in the Crime Control and Safe Streets Act) to hunt criminals with wiretaps and other electronic surveillance. "Unfortunately and unhappily," McClellan reminded Mitchell, outgoing Attorney General Ramsey Clark had refused to implement this part of the law (because, as nobody said, Clark considers wiretaps to be ineffective, poor substitutes for good police work, and inherently dangerous to personal privacy and rights). Mitchell said he will use the power, "carefully and effectively," with full intent "to protect the privacy and rights of individuals."

Senator Philip A. Hart of Michigan, a progressive Democrat,

recalled (in the gentlest possible way) Mr. Nixon's campaign attacks upon "the present Attorney General" and his incessant promises to restore law and order with "a new Attorney General." Remarking that in his opinion Clark had been "a superb Attorney General," Hart asked Mitchell: "How will your administration of the Department of Justice differ from his?" Apart from using the hitherto shunned wiretap power, Mitchell first answered, he really didn't know and wouldn't until he had time to study the department. Later, as if pulling himself together, he said the department would also differ in its more vigorous "pursuit of people engaged in organized crime."

Senator Edward Kennedy asked, very politely, for Mitchell's "general view of the progress we have made in civil rights." Mitchell replied that he applauded the progress—it had begun, after all, in the Eisenhower Administration. In the laws enacted then and since, "the basic weapons are there to protect those rights, and in the administration of present legislation, I propose to do it." School desegregation guidelines were the Department of Health, Education and Welfare's business, not the Department of Justice's, and he would leave them to the HEW Secretary: "I am not familiar with them." Senator Kennedy did not observe, as he might have, that Justice and HEW jointly enforce the guidelines. He settled for a reply, so vague as to be meaningless, to a question about the standards Mitchell was applying in his search, then still without announced results, for his Deputy and Assistant Attorney Generals. What sort of men, with what views, were sought for the civil rights and anti-trust divisions? These questions were not asked.

Senators Kennedy and Hart congratulated Mr. Mitchell, welcomed his appointment. Senator Hiram Fong of Hawaii, the only Republican who even implied a doubt, offered his "warmest congratulations" upon "a very excellent appointment." The new Attorney General, approved by the committee and sure of confirmation, left behind when he departed in his subdued blue suit an impression of an able and stolid man, a man who is good at protecting himself by withholding himself, a true Nixon man.

Command Staff

In the room and at the table where President Nixon sits with his Cabinet, his National Security Council, his Council on Urban Affairs, his Cabinet Committee on Economic Policy, and his Council of Economic Advisers, President Harry S. Truman leaned to his left on September 26, 1947, and touched James Forrestal, the first Secretary of Defense, on the knee. "Now, Jimmy," Truman said, "this is going to be *my* Council." The National Security Act had just been signed, the National Security Council created by it had assembled in the Cabinet Room at the White House for its first meeting, and up to that moment there was doubt as to whether it would be Truman's Council or Forrestal's Council. Forrestal, who was already torn by the inward tensions that would drive him to suicide 18 months later, had arranged office space for the Council secretariat and even for the President's assistant for national security affairs, Admiral Sidney Souers, in a suite next to his own at the Pentagon. He expected as Secretary of Defense to have a major part in formulating foreign as well as military policy, he had less than complete confidence in Mr. Truman's capacity in both spheres, and he saw in the new Council—which a study group appointed by him

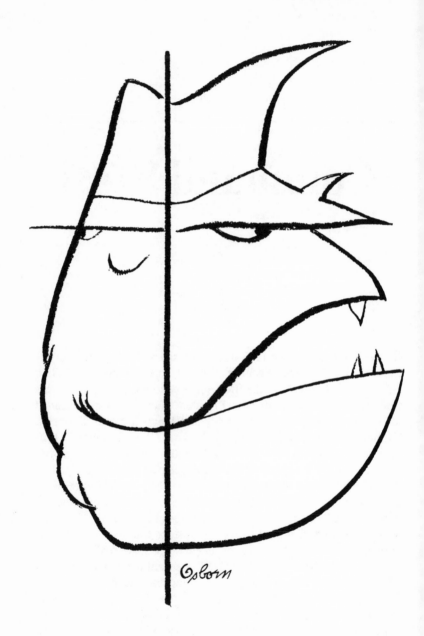

had conceived—a vehicle for asserting the influence on national
policy that he considered himself uniquely qualified to wield.

With the stand he took at that first meeting, Mr. Truman de-
stroyed Forrestal's unreal hopes and made the NSC, then and
ever afterward, in fact what it is in law—the President's Council
and nobody else's. It and its supporting secretariat have been
and can be no more useful than the incumbent President wants
them to be. President Truman, who initially regarded the NSC
as a potential intruder upon his responsibilities and prerogatives,
smothered it with neglect until, in the difficult early months of
the Korean War, he realized that it had acquired a symbolic importance in the public mind and that NSC sanction of unpopular
policies could be helpful. President Eisenhower, with his Army
training, valued the NSC's staff and advisory capabilities as Truman never had. Under Eisenhower, an attached Planning Board
to develop policy, an Operations Coordinating Board to oversee
the implementation of policy, and staffs drawn from State, Defense,
and the CIA to serve the boards and the Council itself over-
flowed from the cramped West Wing of the White House to the
cavernous Executive Office Building across the closed street that
separates the two. President Kennedy, who had a notion that he
and a few aides could run the national security apparatus by
telephone, demolished the entire Eisenhower structure. He allowed
it to be rebuilt on a drastically reduced scale only after the Bay
of Pigs disaster of 1961 awakened him, as the Korean War had
awakened Truman, to the symbolic value of the Council and to
the practical value of its staff organization.

President Johnson used the curtailed NSC setup much as John
Kennedy used it—largely for staff purposes, with less regard than
was publicly pretended for the Council as an advisory body. In
addition to the advisory roles of his successive assistants for
security affairs, McGeorge Bundy and Walt W. Rostow, Mr. Johnson relied upon the NSC staff of some 15 professional anonyms
under Bromley K. Smith, the NSC's executive secretary, to keep
him informed of all that was going on in the departmental laby-
rinths beyond the White House and to see to it, so far as possible,
that his decisions were understood and obeyed by the State, De-

fense, and other bureaucracies involved with foreign policy. Thus the NSC organization that Mr. Nixon inherited was in the main an organization of operators and communicators. It was small; so secret that only the President, his assistant for security affairs, and the executive secretary had anything like adequate knowledge of what it was doing; and vulnerable to criticism for that reason. The symbolic reputation of the Council magnified the vulnerability, as was shown by Mr. Nixon with his absurd allegation during the 1968 campaign that "most of our serious reverses abroad since 1960" were due to neglect of the Council. The primary requirement of any NSC system is that it serve the President as he wants to be served. It is only a mechanism, composed at the Council level of officials (the Vice President, the Secretaries of State and Defense, the seldom noticed Director of Emergency Preparedness, and any others the President may include) who may be consulted in or outside the Council, and composed at the staff level of functionaries who could be available if there were no NSC.

But it would be as silly to underrate the NSC concept and system as it was of Mr. Nixon to overrate it for partisan effect in 1968. He was serious and not at all silly when he said, "I intend to restore the National Security Council to its preeminent role in national security planning." During the first fortnight of his Presidency, he and his assistant for security affairs, Henry A. Kissinger, moved rapidly if somewhat frenetically to fulfill that promise. President Nixon announced that the Council would meet twice weekly until further notice, dealing when feasible with one priority problem at a time (e.g., the Middle East on February 1). The President insisted, in some instances overriding Kissinger's strong objections, that all but three members of the old NSC staff be dismissed forthwith and that only two of them be retained beyond the immediate transition. Mr. Nixon also dictated the tentative reorganization of the staff structure, generally following Kissinger's recommendations but making it very clear indeed that it was to be *his* Council and *his* staff organization, subject to use and change with experience as he, the President, might determine.

Kissinger turned to State, Defense, and the academies for a talented staff—"a real powerhouse," said a departing Johnsonite— that soon totalled 25 substantive officers and later peaked at around 40, nearly three times the number that served Kennedy and Johnson. It was hardly the aggregation of "new faces" that Mr. Nixon seemed to have in mind before he took office, but there are dissenters in every establishment and Mr. Kissinger may have had some of them among his recruits. They included in the beginning such career Foreign Service men as Viron Vaky (Latin America), Helmut Sonnenfeldt (Soviet affairs), Donald Lesh and Robert Houdek (who worked in Dean Rusk's personal secretariat). Morton Halperin, chief of the McNamara-Clifford policy and arms-control planning staff at the Pentagon and a writer of distinction on foreign affairs, was one of three recruits who ranked as deputy assistant secretaries at State and Defense. Another of them was Richard Cooper, a Yale economist and specialist in international monetary affairs. Colonel (later Brigadier General) Alexander M. Haig, formerly a deputy superintendent at the West Point Military Academy, was brought in to record the discussions and decisions at NSC meetings and to assist in NSC staff management. One of Mr. Nixon's campaign advisers, Richard V. Allen, was appointed a senior assistant to Kissinger before the serious work of staff organization began after the Inauguration. A Kremlinologist with stern views on how to counter Soviet and Chinese Communist power, he took some lumps from columnists and was subsequently put under wraps in an office well removed from Kissinger's.

During the first fortnight, the NSC-Kissinger area in the White House basement bulged with new staffers who had neither offices, desks nor secretaries, worked on sofas, and had to confer with visitors in a teeming hallway. Kissinger's secretary laughed madly when a telephone caller asked for the secretary to Lawrence Eagleburger, a Foreign Service officer who had been assigned to Nixon headquarters in New York during the pre-Inaugural transition and so impressed Kissinger that he was appointed the head man's executive assistant. Eagleburger, it developed, had a small desk in what had been the foyer outside the Kissinger office and a secretary would have had to sit on his lap. Richard Moose, co-author of a critical analysis of the Kennedy-Johnson operation, had been moved in with the outgoing executive secretary, Bromley Smith, giving rise to the supposition that Moose was destined to succeed Smith.

The staff structure approved and to some extent imposed by President Nixon is divided into three functional segments—"the operators," "the planners," and "the programmers." The "operators" do for Mr. Nixon what the previous staff did for Mr. Johnson, drawing into the White House a mass of departmental information, sorting from it items that should concern the President, and conveying his instructions and reactions to the departments. The "planners" do some original planning of their own, but their principal assignment is to stimulate more and better planning at State and Defense—a task that was undertaken with gusto and resulted in those departments being flooded in the early period with demands for reassessments and justifications of present policy and for new policy approaches. The "programmers" are supposed to bridge the geographic and jurisdictional lines that divide most policy functions (Africa from the Far East and Europe, economic aid from military aid, State from Defense) and to view policy problems and programs on a global basis. They are also intended to bridge the gap between the planners and the operators, both at the White House and in the departments, trying to see that the planners don't get too far from immediate needs and that the operators don't get lost in current complications and detail.

At a "background" session with Kissinger in December of 1968, reporters got the impression that an Eisenhower-style Planning Board was to be reestablished as an important NSC adjunct and manned, as before, by assistant secretaries from State and Defense and their equivalents from CIA and the Treasury. The nearest thing to a Planning Board in the actual structure is a new Review Group, chaired by Kissinger and including senior departmental officials. It is what the name suggests, a group reviewing policy proposals on their way up from the departments to the Council and the President, rather than originating policy within the NSC system. A "Committee of Under Secretaries," headed by the Under Secretary of State, replaced the Senior Inter-departmental Group (SIG) established in 1966 by President Johnson in the hope, never satisfactorily realized, that it would have Presidential policy implemented as the President intended it to be. The subordinate Interdepartmental Regional Groups (IRG's), also set up in 1966 to implement policy at their levels, were retained, but with a difference of the kind that seems terribly important to policy bureaucrats. The old IRG's were headed by State Department chairmen and reported to the White House through department channels. The revised IG's report directly to Kissinger and function as components of the NSC system rather than as satellites of State.

Those who described the Nixon system acknowledged that it was fuzzy at the start. There was about it a tinge of change for the sake of change. But the stated purpose behind the changes was good. It was to identify for the President all of the alternatives that are practicably open to him in a given situation; to see that they go up to him through the Council in clear and actionable form; and to assure that his choices, once they have been thrashed out in the Council and made by him, are conveyed back to the bureaucracies in clear and actionable form. This had been the intended purpose of every NSC system devised since 1947 and the purpose had never been accomplished to the full satisfaction of any President.

What comes clear is that the Nixon NSC staff is not fundamentally designed to be either a planning staff or an operating staff (although Kissinger eventually placed more emphasis upon in-house planning than he initially did). It is a command staff, through which President Nixon undertakes to fasten and keep a firm grip upon the departments, primarily State and Defense, that apply or misapply his policies.

V

Discipline and Order

The Reverend Billy Graham knew whereof he spoke when he said in his prayer at the Nixon Inaugural that this President needs more help than any previous President has required. For mundane help, as distinct from the divine aid besought for him by his favorite evangelist, Mr. Nixon has installed at the White House and in the adjacent Executive Office Building the biggest and most elaborate array of assistants, assistants to assistants, councils and sub-councils in Presidential history. During his first three weeks in office, President Nixon devoted more time and energy to the organization of his staff, and to making sure that the principal members of it understood exactly what they were and were not expected to do for him, than to any other subject or problem. Disciplined order and precision within his immediate establishment, he seemed to realize, was a prerequisite to the promise and appearance of orderly administration that he succeeded from the start in conveying to the country.

Evidently to further the image of both an orderly and an "open" Administration, the President and his assistant for national security affairs, Henry A. Kissinger, took the unprecedented step on February 7 of announcing not only the structure but the personnel of an enlarged and reorganized National Security Council secretariat. It is as I described it earlier, except that Mr. Nixon finally allowed Kissinger to retain six rather than only two of the 15 NSC staffers who sufficed for President Johnson. Comparable expansion for a comparable reason—President Nixon's determination to assert and establish effective command over the whole Executive Branch of the federal government—occurred with less notice and disclosure on the domestic side of the Nixon setup. The home-side organization is in some respects more interesting, in that it is more revealing of Mr. Nixon and his approach to his Presidency, than the publicized NSC and foreign-policy organization is.

The most interesting of Mr. Nixon's early additions to the standard White House administrative system was his appointment of the first "Counsellor to the President." The President's announcement identified the Counsellor, Arthur F. Burns, as "a longtime friend and trusted advisor," granted him Cabinet rank, and said that his role "will be that of a generalist, dealing with a broad province (*sic*) of legislative and executive actions." This was an understatement. Mr. Burns, who was President Eisenhower's first chairman of the Council of Economic Advisers and ex-officio ad-

viser afterward to both Eisenhower and Vice President Nixon, was asked on the day of his new appointment whether his wide juris-diction would conflict with that of his friend and protege, Paul McCracken, chairman of the Nixon Council of Economic Advisers. Burns thought not. "My range," he said, "is very much wider than economics. . . . However, I would not be discharging my responsi-bilities if I stayed out of this sphere of economics. I will be in there inevitably."

Mr. Burns has been and will be "in there" across the whole sweep of the President's policy and administrative concerns. One of his tasks, as he sees it, is to detect and resolve disputed issues of policy and administration before they become the President's problems. It is a conception that requires high officials, Cabinet members included, to recognize his primacy and to accept his intervention without appeal to President Nixon, and Burns is aware of the potential for jealousy and discord inherent in it. He relies upon his known standing with the President and upon a general acceptance of his assurances that he has no wish to build a White House empire for himself to avert trouble of that kind. In his first weeks on the job—he functioned as "Counsellor" before the ap-pointment was announced—he refereed a bitter jurisdictional dis-pute between two agency heads (unidentified); tightened up the procedures for review of the fiscal 1970 budget inherited from President Johnson; recommended to the President, at Paul Mc-Cracken's request, steps to give more responsibility and "visibility" to McCracken's colleagues on the Council of Economic Advisers, Herbert Stein and Hendrick Houthakker; and sparked a pro-digious number of Presidential orders to departments and agencies to review existing policies and practices and come up with new ones. He also is in charge of preparing what he calls "a significant program of legislation" for submission to Congress, he takes a hand in determining the agenda for Cabinet meetings, and he is busy finding things for the new Cabinet Committee on Economic Policy to do that the Council of Economic Advisers is not doing.

Counsellor Burns obviously needs, and he has, a staff of his own. His deputy is one of the President's special assistants, 31-year-old Martin Anderson, a Columbia University economist and authority on urban problems who is actively involved, on Burns' behalf, with the new Council on Urban Affairs and its numerous sub-councils. Wesley McCain, another young Columbia economist, assists Anderson. The presence of two other staffers seems rather odd, but Burns insists that it isn't. They are Richard Burress, a Washington lawyer who until recently was counsel to the House (of Representatives) Republican Policy Committee, and Jack Tom Cole, former legislative assistant to Republican Senator John Tower of Texas. They are said to be skilled drafters of legislation, to have inside knowledge of Republican and Congressional politics that Burns finds useful, and in no way to be duplicating the work of Bryce N. Harlow, the assistant for Congressional relations, and his staff.

Another Nixon generalist, former Congressman Robert Ellsworth of Kansas, understands that he may be assigned to work for the President "in any area, anywhere in government or the world." He figured importantly in the prelude to Mr. Nixon's recent suspension of the Johnson order granting and denying new Pacific routes to competing airlines. Just now Ellsworth is trying to reconcile candidate Nixon's promises to give the Southern textile industry more protection against imports with President Nixon's Inaugural commitment to the ideal of "an open world—open to ideas, open to the exchange of goods and people." He also has a continuing assignment, one that could get him and the President into trouble if it is mishandled. It is to keep tabs for the President upon the doings of some 15 independent agencies and regulatory commissions. Ellsworth, for example, will be expected to forewarn the President of such developments as the Federal Communications Commission's proposal to ban all TV and radio advertising of cigarettes. How to accomplish this without seeming to evince White House interest in particular cases or to be interfering improperly in other ways with the agencies he is instructed to watch is a problem that Mr. Nixon expects Ellsworth to solve for himself. In dealing with it and in his other work, he has the assistance of a California mathematician, C. T. Whitehouse; a young New York investment adviser, Daniel Hofgren; and a young Ohio lawyer, Jonathan Rose.

A team of eight writer-researchers has been a good deal more tightly structured than the stars on it anticipated when they worked for Mr. Nixon's nomination and election. James Keogh, a former *Time* editor, is their editor and supervisor, and he runs a taut shop.

Drafts of speeches, proclamations, other Presidential statements are supposed to be on Keogh's desk by 3 p.m. of the day before Mr. Nixon is to use them. Each man has a specific though not exclusive assignment—Keogh to the Cabinet, Raymond K. Price to Urban Affairs, William Safire to the Cabinet Committee on Economic Policy, Patrick Buchanan to White House meetings with Congressional leaders. Buchanan, a former editorial writer who has worked for Mr. Nixon since 1966 and got more notice than he wanted during the 1968 campaign as the candidate's favorite conservative, and Tom Huston, a junior assistant, are responsible for a daily summary and analysis of newspaper, magazine, radio and TV news and comment, which is delivered to Mr. Nixon every morning. Whatever a President thinks he needs is automatically considered to be worthwhile, but Pat Buchanan's considerable talents seem to be wasted on such a chore. Ray Price, who wrote more of Mr. Nixon's policy speeches than anyone else on the preelection team, has a flair for and knowledge of foreign affairs that cannot be of much use at Urban Council meetings. Buchanan, Price, and the other veterans of the staff rank third in the Nixon pecking order of "assistants," "deputy assistants," "special assistants," and "staff assistants" to the President. The theory is that they will contribute to the evolution of policy in their assigned fields, but one gets the impression around the White House that they find themselves farther from the President and less involved in the policy process than they had hoped to be.

The senior Negro on the Nixon staff is Robert J. Brown, a thirty-three year old former policeman, Treasury agent, and High Point, N.C., public-relations man who has the title of "special assistant." He has just hired two "staff assistants," a New York lawyer, Bruce Rabb, white, and James Sexton, a Negro who had been specializing in minority problems at the Commerce Department. Bob Brown likes to think of himself as a Nixon generalist and says that only 20 percent of his time so far has been spent on Negro and other minority matters. His associates and the President have a different impression. At the suggestion of Roy Wilkins, director of the NAACP, Nixon dispatched Mr. Brown to Mississippi to check on what, if anything, was being done for the black victims of a tornado at Hazlehurst and a butane gas explosion at Laurel. Mr. Brown was summoned from his Washington home on a recent Saturday evening to mollify a group of disgruntled Negro leaders who had been ignored when they appeared at a White House gate with demands to be enlightened on what Mr. Nixon meant with his talk of "black capitalism." After a night meeting with them at a motel, Mr. Brown felt that he had reassured if not entirely satisfied them.

The word that Mr. Brown is at the White House to look after black and other minority interests has apparently been spread with more effect through the country at large than it has in Washington. He said the other day (without complaint) that nobody in official-dom had consulted him about Nixon policy on school desegrega-tion, for instance. Mrs. Ruby Martin, who refused to stay on at the Department of Health, Education, and Welfare as chief of its civil rights office, said after she had decided to leave that she had never heard of Robert Brown. She supposed that Pat Buchanan and Deputy Assistant Harry Dent, Senator Strom Thur-mond's man in the office of White House Counsel John Ehrlichman, had more than anybody else at the White House to do with her policy area. When he was told that a good many Negroes in Wash-ington and elsewhere are still looking for a friend at the White House, Mr. Brown said, "Tell 'em that my door is open and to come and see me." He displays with pride letters from several black militants. One of them wrote to him from Boston, "What a joy it is to know of your appointment. It is a good move for soul people."

President Nixon's leading in-house liberal—a description that some liberals question—is his assistant for urban affairs, Daniel Patrick Moynihan. Apart from his large and sobering responsibili-ties for the work of the Cabinet-level Council on Urban Affairs, Moynihan provides a dash of verbal salt and pepper that nobody else around the Nixon White House dares or cares to supply. His references to "the ferocious Mr. Ziegler" (Press Secretary Ronald Ziegler) and to the latter's imagined desire that he, Moynihan, "get the hell out of here before I make some more mistakes" were deleted from the transcript of an early press briefing. His later remark that "the nut-cutting issue" within the Administration is divvying up the billions that may or may not be available for social purposes, once the Vietnam war is ended, remained on the briefing record.

Mr. Moynihan, whose long Irish face resembles a cross between the late Winston Churchill and a weeping hound, said when he went to work at the White House that his staff was going to be "young, integrated, and bushy-tailed," and it is. The one Negro on it so far is Michael C. Monroe, 31, a former Cowles Magazines editor who worked on Nixon's campaign press staff in New York and, along with his more serious concern with minority problems, handles press relations for the Urban Council. The senior deputy to Moynihan is Stephen Hess, 35, co-author of a current and admired book, *The Republican Establishment* and of an earlier biography of Nixon. John Price, 30, a lawyer and the Moynihan staff's counsel and general manager, and Christopher DeMuth, 22, are former officials of that bastion of liberal Republican dissent, the Ripon Society. Richard Blumenthal, 22, and Harvard '68, came to Moynihan from the *Washington Post*. The old man of the staff is Leonard S. Zartman, 42 (Moynihan's age), who quit his job as an Eastman Kodak attorney for a piece of the Nixon action, Moynihan style.

Ronald Ziegler, the victim of Moynihan's friendly jibes, has surprised his friends in the Nixon press corps with his firm conduct of the Press Secretary's job and office. When the going got rough during the 1968 campaign, he and his famously proficient press staff tended to crack a bit. There has been no sign of that since the Inauguration. It is as if Ziegler, aged 30, a sometime account executive in the J. Walter Thompson advertising agency's Los Angeles office and a volunteer worker for Nixon in earlier campaigns, had taken on a little of the Presidency's prestige and authority. Everyone who deals with him and his four assistants knows that the real authority in press matters rests with Herbert Klein, the President's Director of Communications, and with the President himself. But Ziegler has adjusted to this fact without diminishing himself and his job. Although he is one of the four or five staffers whose duties require them to see the President in person several times a day, he possesses and conveys none of the personal authority that gave weight to the pronouncements, public and private, of such recent predecessors as Bill D. Moyers and Pierre Salinger. His value to the press and to his boss lies simply in the fact that whatever he says, however little, is known to be precisely what President Nixon wants said for him.

Ziegler is wholly frank about this. "I would never say anything at a briefing unless I'd checked it with the President," he says, and he does check at frequent intervals. According to Ziegler and others at the White House, Mr. Nixon does not react to his press and television notices, favorable and otherwise, with the ferocity that made many an exciting moment during the Kennedy and Johnson regimes. But the accompanying pretense that Mr. Nixon really doesn't care, one way or the other, is nonsense. He often mentions the pain that cutting cartoons give him and his family, he sprinkles his press conferences and less formal appearances with references to various reporters and their work, and he manages himself in the Presidency with conscious and close regard for public effect. Ziegler's job essentially is to speak within limits for his President without ever standing between the President and the President's audience.

Leaving H. R. (Bob) Haldeman to the last in any account of the Nixon White House is likely to be regarded as heresy there. He, one of his junior assistants (Lawrence Higby), Ziegler and Dwight Chapin, a lacquered young man who sees Mr. Nixon's office visitors in and out and performs other personal services, are all recruits from the Thompson agency. Haldeman, their senior in years and rank, is commonly called the President's Chief of Staff— "the boss of this whole shebang," another assistant puts it. He and his recently appointed deputy, retired Air Force Colonel Alexander Butterfield, clear every individual and every piece of paper on their way to the President's office. The paper is checked beforehand by a sub-staff of five headed by Special Assistant Kenneth R. Cole, Jr. Haldeman is one of the few Nixon aides-in-chief who so far have officially banned all communication and contact with the working press—until, he tells his own staff, "we get shaken down." I don't mind, and readers shouldn't, either. Bob Haldeman and his seven assistants are efficient functionaries, no more. For what really matters at the Nixon White House, the wise inquirer will turn, probably with limited success, to such advisers in the actual stream of power as Henry Kissinger and Counsellor Burns.

VI

Balancing Act

Just before the 91st Congress convened in early January, 1969, I asked Senator Everett M. Dirksen of Illinois to clarify news accounts of his attitude toward two of his Republican colleagues and their rival ambitions to assist him in his role as the Senate Minority Leader. Senator Dirksen had been the Minority Leader since 1959 and—reelected in 1968 to his fourth Senate term at age 72— he was sure to retain the floor leadership without opposition when the 43 Republican Senators in this Congress met in secret caucus. For the first time since 1959, however, there was a contest for the assistant leadership. The former assistant, or "Whip," Senator Thomas H. Kuchel of California, had been defeated for renomination and another Republican of moderate persuasion, Hugh Scott of Pennsylvania, was opposing Roman L. Hruska of Nebraska for the vacated post. Senator Dirksen had not announced a preference for either of them. He was known to favor Hruska, but the news reports had him lending his man only "tacit support" and acting as if he didn't much care who won. Did he care and, if he did, why? He answered: "I am a conservative. Mr. Hruska is a conservative. Mr. Hruska is more nearly in line with my thinking. This country has elected a President whom I regard

as a conservative. I don't think you need any more than that, do you?"

As it turned out, a majority of the new Senate's Republicans decided that they needed considerably more than that. They elected Senator Scott and rejected Senator Hruska, 23 to 20. The event was overshadowed in public interest by Edward M. Kennedy's sudden and successful drive to unseat the Democratic Whip, Russell Long of Louisiana, but the Republican choice probably tells more about the Senate Republicans as they line up for the first Nixon years than the Kennedy victory tells about the Democrats.

For an understanding of what Scott over Hruska means, we have to go back to 1959 and to the circumstances that led the 35 Republicans then in the Senate to choose Kuchel, the California maverick, for their Whip at the same time they elected Dirksen, who at the time was even more conservative than he is now, their leader-in-chief. The Republican liberals (the term is used in a relative sense) had put up John Sherman Cooper of Kentucky for leader and Kuchel for his assistant; the conservatives, Dirksen and Senator Karl Mundt of South Dakota. Dirksen won as expected, 21 to 14, and his forces were set to elect Mundt when Senator George D. Aiken of Vermont intervened. In his fourth term— he was reelected in 1968 to his sixth—he argued as he had many times in the past that the Republican party was committing national suicide with its tendency, personified by the Dirksen-Mundt combination, to let its "extreme right-wing conservatives" monopolize the leadership. A Senator who was present recalls, perhaps with some exaggeration, that the usually quiet and gentle Aiken told Dirksen, Mundt, and their leader-in-fact, the late Styles Bridges of New Hampshire, "If you do this, it will be war to the death. You'll never draw another peaceful breath." Aiken said enough to convince Bridges that the imposition of Dirksen *and* Mundt upon the moderate faction would irretrievably split the party in the Senate. Bridges passed the word and Kuchel won by the same vote that Dirksen had received. Dirksen squelched a tentative move to replace Kuchel in 1966 and there probably would have been no contest if Kuchel had returned. With him out, the Dirksen conservatives figured that one of their own, Senator Hruska, could be installed without the disruptive effects of ousting a moderate incumbent.

By the accepted canons of Senate conduct, Mr. Hruska deserved to win. Appointed to the Senate in 1954 and twice elected to full terms, he is respected by his moderate-to-liberal colleagues, Republican and Democratic, for his dogged energy, his unspectacular but recognized talents as a lawyer and legislator, and—a quality noted with a certain admiration by his fellows—his unexcelled capacity for couching cogent points in ponderous language. In person, he is a warm and likable man. In his public guise, he is among the dullest of the dull. The super-conservative Americans for Constitutional Action annoys him year after year with ratings of 95 to a perfect 100 on its "consistency index" (he was the only Senator who scored 100 with ACA in 1968). His votes in 1968 displeased *The New Republic* on 11 of 12 significant issues, and he finishes near the bottom of Americans for Democratic Action ratings. He has voted against every authorization and appropriation for foreign economic aid since he entered the Senate. He has worked, usually in collaboration with Senator Dirksen, to water down every civil rights bill enacted since 1957 and, also with Dirksen, has voted for all of them in their final versions. He has similarly worked and voted to diminish and then to pass, though with less consistency, some poverty and urban renewal legislation. He has originated several measures aimed at penal reform and the humane treatment of narcotics addicts and, with at least equal zeal, has cosponsored tough anti-crime laws that rely heavily upon wiretaps and other covert surveillance. Last year, in the wake of the King and Kennedy assassinations, he withstood a flood of Nebraska letters opposing any control whatever over gun sales and, as one of the Judiciary Committee's most industrious members, helped to narrow and then to pass an act imposing limited federal controls.

Senator Scott offers a fairly complete contrast, both in personality and record. At 68, four years older than Senator Hruska, Senator Scott has the verve of a much younger man (his age is not mentioned in his official biographical sketches). He is witty; a collector of Chinese art; fast on his feet, and, when he wishes to be, cutting in debate. He rated a minus 41 (printed in red) on ACA's 1968 index and suited *The New Republic* with eight of 12 votes on selected issues. Senator Scott supported, Senator Hruska opposed two proposals by a staunch conservative, Senator John Williams of Delaware, to hold down subsidy payments to wealthy farmers. Scott opposed, Hruska supported four amendments that would have pretty well gutted the open-housing sections of the 1968 Civil Rights Act. Hruska supported, Scott opposed two attempts to cut the funds appropriated for model cities and urban renewal. But Senator Scott voted with Senator Hruska against three efforts to delete or modify the wiretap authority granted to federal officials in the Crime Control and Safe Streets Act, and both of them supported a Dirksen amendment allotting most of the funds authorized for improving police forces and practices to the states to spend as they choose. Hruska opposed, Scott supported a proposal to delay the construction of an anti-ballistic missile system, but both of them voted against a more stringent proposal to eliminate ABM funds from the defense budget. Both also opposed extending the life of the Arms Control and Disarmament Agency for more than one year.

The fact that 23 of this year's 43 Republican Senators preferred Senator Scott with his record to Senator Hruska with his record speaks for itself. But there was more to the vote for Whip than that. Six of the nine new Republican Senators (excluding Barry Goldwater, who was returning to the Senate after his 1964 debacle, and Charles Goodell of New York, who was appointed in time to take his seat at the last session), voted for Scott. Eleven of the 17 Republicans elected or appointed in the past two years preferred him to Roman Hruska. Senator Hruska, confident of victory up to the hour of voting, had counted on the support of at least three of the freshman Senators (Marlow Cook of Kentucky, Robert Packwood of Oregon, and William Saxbe of Ohio) who went to Scott. But the harshest blow to Senator Hruska and his patron, Senator Dirksen, was the vote of four of the Senate's six senior Republicans. Of the six, only Karl Mundt and Dirksen himself voted for Hruska. Senator Aiken, senior of them all, was expected to vote for Scott and did (he seconded Scott's nomination in the caucus). The second and third Senators in length of service, Milton Young of North Dakota and John Williams of Delaware, and Margaret Chase Smith of Maine (fifth), also chose Scott over Hruska. They haven't said why, but it may be supposed that they remembered the 1959 showdown between Mundt and Kuchel, and

George Aiken's warning, and considered that it applied even more forcefully now than it had then. Senator Young promised his vote to Scott soon after Kuchel was defeated. A conservative by most ratings and "a little right of center" by his own, he was said to feel that the moderate wing represented by Senator Scott should retain the second spot in plain fairness and, more importantly, because of the impression the country would gather from the vote.

Senator Aiken, who is as wise as they come on Capitol Hill, said afterward:

I had in mind the effect the result would have on the country. I felt it very important that we not give the image to the country that the very conservative wing controls the party, and by control I mean monopolizes the party and the leadership. The conservative wing had the power to take over, to monopolize the party in the Senate completely. The question was, did they have the judgment not to do it? They did have the power, and they had the wisdom not to do it.

Of Senator Hruska: "He has the ability, he likes to work, he attends to his work. But there was the feeling that he was put forward by the extreme right wing of the party."

And put forward, though Senator Aiken was too courteous to say so, by Senator Dirksen. The cruel truth is that a good many Senators, veteran conservatives among them, were fed up with Mr. Dirksen's leadership. His changeable ways, usually attributed by the press to an admirable flexibility and wiliness, had caused acute embarrassment to Senators who were prepared to follow him in (for example) opposition to the consular treaty with the Soviet Union, only to find him suddenly for it; or, for another recent instance, federal rent supplements, which he marshalled the Republican troops to oppose and then commanded them to support on a reduced scale. Conservative Senator Williams of Delaware, in an open letter aimed at the departed Senator Kuchel, who was not renowned for his industry on the floor, but by implication also at Senator Dirksen, touched upon another source of complaint. Because the floor leaders were often too busy to be on the floor, he had observed situations "where there would be no Republican Senator on the floor during the discussions of major bills." The remedy, he rather unkindly added, might be the election this year of an assistant leader who was junior in both service and age to either Scott or Hruska.

Beneath the surface of customary Senatorial courtesy, it was not an altogether gentlemanly struggle. Scott, Hruska, and Dirksen asked some of the freshmen what their committee preferences were —just idle curiosity, of course. The freshmen's votes actually made little or no difference in their committee assignments; those who voted for Scott fared as well as the three who voted for Hruska. It was said of Senator Hruska that "he lives under Senator Dirksen's armpit" and of Senator Scott that some of his non-friends in Pennsylvania call him "Potty Scotty—because he won't get off the pot."

That sort of thing was rare, by the way. What mattered was that a majority of Republican Senators, probably including quite a few of the 20 who voted for Hruska (19, really, since Hruska and Scott voted for themselves), were genuinely concerned about the party's image. One gathered, hearing the word so often in explanation of the vote, that they may be more concerned with the image than with the substance behind it. But the concern is constructive if it implies a preference for the moderate image projected by Senator Scott rather than the one cast by Senator Dirksen when he said: "I am a conservative. Mr. Hruska is a conservative."

———

After the death of Senator Dirksen on September 7, Senator Hruska withdrew from a contest with Senator Scott for the minority leadership and another moderate, Robert Griffin of Michigan, succeeded Scott as the deputy leader. One suspects that at times since then Mr. Nixon would have been glad to trade improvement in the GOP image for party discipline of a kind that Senators Scott and Griffin have neither imposed nor practiced.

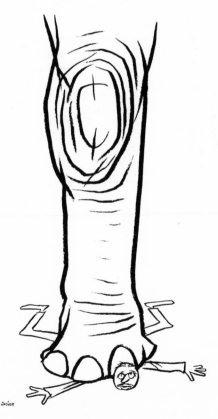

VII

The 91st Congress

As the new Administration enters its third month, Congress is still "waiting for Nixon," and both Republicans and Democrats are beginning to wonder why the President is taking so long to formulate and submit a domestic legislative program. The line that the slow pace merely reflects the President's "careful wending of his way," as House Republican leader Gerald Ford tells his restive band, is wearing thin. The Democrats audibly doubt that he knows the way he wants to go and Republicans in frequent touch with him are embarrassed by their patent lack of certain knowledge that he does. The embarrassment extends to the White House, where concern that the vaunted Nixon prudence may soon be taken for procrastination is evident among his staff.

After the Republican leadership's regular Tuesday meeting with Mr. Nixon on March 24, Congressman Ford and his Senate counterpart, Everett Dirksen, took obvious pleasure in their ability to announce that there *will* be an Administration bill to curb one-bank holding companies. They could say as much about very little else in the domestic area. Even the Nixon position on retaining the ten percent surtax on incomes was in doubt: Senator Dirksen could and did recite all of the familiar reasons, many of them previously noted by the President, why abandoning the surtax this year is just about impossible, but he had not been authorized to say that the Administration intends to recommend its retention. At his two sessions to date with the Congressional leaders of both parties—he has had no serious discussion with the Democrats alone—Mr. Nixon has talked only in generalities that left the majority leaders on whom he must depend for legislative success more irritated than pleased. Two of his Cabinet secretaries, Robert Finch of HEW and George Shultz of Labor, have been busy on Capitol Hill in group and individual conversations with strategically placed Representatives and Senators, and they have cultivated the liberal-to-moderate Democrats with special zeal. Their message has been that Nixon is coming up with a domestic program that all but the wildest liberals can support, and that even they can accept without excessive pain. When the Cabinet emissaries are asked to get specific, however—"Okay, but what's he going to do?" —they have had to answer that they don't know what Mr. Nixon is going to do about specific issues, because Mr. Nixon hasn't told them, either.

Granting that the pros and cons of every major domestic issue confronting the President are being studied and weighed with all the deliberate care claimed by the Nixon staff, another and relevant explanation is also offered privately at the White House. It is that Mr. Nixon is getting two contradictory readings of the dominant attitudes in the 91st Congress and particularly in the House of Representatives. The one with the heaviest professional backing is that he faces in this Congress the same coalition of conservative Democrats and rock-hard Republicans that Lyndon Johnson had to deal with, and that any significant domestic legislation with a chance of passage will have to be tailored for that coalition. The other reading is that there is in the House, ready and anxious for Presidential encouragement, the makings of a majority coalition of more or less liberal Republicans and liberal-to-moderate Democrats that could, if intelligently recognized and nurtured, assure passage of the kind of legislation that Finch, Shultz, and Nixon himself profess to prefer. It seems clear that what Mr. Nixon wants above all else from this Congress is a successful first session, successful at least in the sense that he survives it without any severe defeats. That requires a correct choice between the two readings offered him, and the impression is that he has yet to decide which of them is the correct one. Once he does decide, this interpretation of the current delay suggests, the Nixon program will be submitted in short order.

Obvious support for the first reading of House attitudes, and less obvious but persuasive support for the second, is to be found in a document that deserves and presumably is receiving close study at the White House. It is an analysis of Democratic voting patterns in the last Congress, published this month by the liberal

Democratic Study Group. The DSG consists of 120 dues-paying Representatives plus 20 to 25 others who generally vote a liberal line but dare not offend their conservative constituents by open association with it. The dues (raised this year from $50 to $100 annually) and private contributions support a small research staff and finance studies like the one published March 10. Its purpose is to show Democrats in the House what the sacred seniority system of selecting committee and subcommittee chairmen actually does to them and to their party, but it has some lessons for Republicans and for the Nixon Administration as well.

The study analyzes votes on 30 key issues in the two sessions of the 90th Congress. The Johnson Administration took a clear position on 26 of the 30 issues, the Democratic party platform on most of them, and in DSG's opinion all of them presented unmistakable choices between liberal and conservative views. Ninety-one percent of the votes cast by DSG Democrats supported the Administration and party position. Only 69 percent of the votes cast by non-DSG Democrats supported their President and party. But the thrust of the study was at the votes of 42 of the 114 Democratic chairmen of committees and subcommittees in the last Congress. The 42, most of them from the South and border states, and all of them beneficiaries of seniority, voted more often against than for the Administration and party position. Thirty-four of the 42 voted more often (92 percent) against Democratic measures than the Republicans did (76 percent). What DSG calls "the national Democratic position"—usually, the declared Democratic Administration position—was defeated in 17 of the 30 instances and "Democratic committee and subcommittee chairmen alone were responsible for over half [of] the 17 defeats." Including the recalcitrant chairmen, 75 non-DSG Democrats voted more often against than for Democratic positions. "All but two of these were conservative to ultra-conservative members from Southern and border states."

The vices and results of rigid adherence to seniority aside, the study is a reminder that a House coalition of Republicans and what a prominent DSG Congressman calls "Republicans with a Southern accent" prevailed on 17 of the 30 tested issues and on many others as well. Because the 1968 elections made very little difference in the composition and membership of the House, the same coalition could be expected to prevail at this session and to threaten any moderate-to-liberal legislation Nixon may have in mind. But a different projection is possible, and some influential Congressmen of both parties hope that Nixon will perceive that it is and act accordingly. Given a liberal core of around 140 DSG Democrats, 50 to 60 others who are inclined that way with less consistency, and the pressures on all Republicans to support their President in his first encounters with Congress, the makings of a moderate coalition are apparent—*if,* the argument runs, the President has the wisdom and the courage to give it a program around which its potential supporters can rally without undue regard for party among the Democrats.

There are interesting signs that this Congress does challenge
Nixon to choose the moderate option. Wilbur Mills of Arkansas,
chairman of the House Ways and Means Committee and one of
DSG's prime targets, has been engaged since February 18 in hearings aimed at broad reform of the federal tax structure along lines
that House and Senate liberals have advocated for years. He is
said to be ready to give priority, with prospects of early action,
to changes in present law that would deprive corporate conglom-

middle of the Roadism

erates and questionable foundations of the tax privileges that they
now enjoy and frequently abuse. Like the Johnson Administration,
the Nixon Administration has taken no position on these and other
proposals before the Mills committee, but Treasury witnesses will
be appearing at the end of the hearings, probably after the Easter
recess, and will then be compelled to declare the Nixon view. Such
conservative stalwarts as Senator Roman Hruska of Nebraska are
preparing their constituents for a Nixon course directed down "the
middle of the road"—veering a little to the right, perhaps, but not
to the ultra-conservative right. Barry Goldwater is admonishing
worried conservative Republican groups not to demand of or

expect from this Republican who won the Presidency all that they expected from the Goldwater who lost it. In early hearings and votes on renewal and extension of the Elementary and Secondary Education Act, the Democratic majority on the House Education and Labor Committee has put Secretary Finch and, through him, the President on notice that any tendency to gut federal programs in that field will be resisted and probably defeated.

If Nixon is getting accurate signals from Capitol Hill, he is aware that much more delay in submitting his major legislation can only make trouble for his Administration. Such disparate and influential Democrats as Hale Boggs of Louisiana, the House majority leader, and Richard Bolling of Missouri, a DSG pillar and advocate of reforming the party's seniority structure, are beginning to wonder whether Mr. Nixon is playing tricks with Congress. Could it be that he intends, by going slow with his proposals and finally submitting very few of any real substance, to encourage Congress to do as little as possible and then, in the 1970 campaign, to blame a "do nothing" Democratic majority in both houses for the poor showing? A suspicion that he has precisely that in mind is much alive among Congressional Democrats and it seems to some of them that their Republican colleagues are singularly embarrassed when it is voiced to them. Neither the Democratic leadership nor the DSG liberals propose to stand still for any such tactic. The DSG plans to establish task forces, supported by expert staff, to develop liberal Democratic legislation that should, at the least, require the Administration to take positions for or against it. The regular leadership is similarly inclined, with the result that the final consequence of dilatory Republican tactics could be that the Nixon Administration rather than the Democratic majority is made to appear as the "do nothing" element in the political equations of 1970 and 1972.

At the close of the first session of the 91st Congress, Mr. Nixon still had not made a clear choice of the options indicated here. His domestic program, not submitted until mid-summer and after, could have been made more appealing to moderates than to conservatives. But the President usually avoided postures that would offend conservative Congressmen and their constituents, and so, by evident design, forfeited without explicitly rejecting the moderate-to-liberal bipartisan coalition that was his for the having.

VIII

Feeling the Heat

At the turn of March into April, the Nixon White House was on the defensive for the first time since the President took office. His assistants sensed and said that he was "feeling the heat" from Congress and from the press for some convincing action, legislative and executive, on the domestic front. They also sensed, and loyally tried to conceal, a certain indecision in the President himself; a tendency, continuing in the third month of his Administration, to grasp at one excuse after another to postpone his choices among alternatives that had, in many instances, been pretty well defined for him before inauguration.

Outwardly as cool and calm as ever, Mr. Nixon had begun to blame others, including the senior dignitary on his staff, Counsellor Arthur F. Burns, for defects in the Presidential decision process and to seek, by changes in that process, to make the appearance of White House order and efficiency the reality that it had never actually been. Bryce N. Harlow, one of the few assistants who knew what Washington was like before the President brought them to the White House in January, perceived a rising unease among his associates and tried to allay it with assurances that less had been accomplished in the initial months of the first Eisenhower term than in the first Nixon months. Another assistant with past knowledge of Washington, former Congressman Robert Ellsworth of Kansas, already wanted out and was said to be impatiently awaiting an ambassadorship. Mr. Nixon's in-house Democrat, former Assistant Secretary of Labor Daniel P. Moynihan, was in such obvious doubt that a defensible program in his field of urban affairs would at last emerge that some people were wondering how long he would stick with the Administration. It had to be and was said for him that he knew "the worst that could happen" in the way of an urban effort short of his hopes and was prepared to live with it and Mr. Nixon until further notice.

The word during the week of April 7 was that things would be changing. Press Secretary Ronald Ziegler, the President's faithful oral reflector, quoted Mr. Nixon to the effect that the work of preparing a domestic program was "moving along as he intended it to move along" and that "we are now moving into the final decision period on these matters." The results, in messages to Congress and in executive announcements, would begin to appear as soon as Congress returned from its Easter recess on April 14. But the only certainty, the only firm decision last week was that there would be no inclusive "package of domestic legislation." In what form to present "the overall domestic program" was also undecided, although Counsellor Burns had prepared and taken to the President, at his Florida retreat in Key Biscayne for the Easter season, the draft outline of a broad program. Burns' session there with the President—along with Harlow, Moynihan, HEW Secretary Robert H. Finch, and White House Counsel John Ehrlichman—produced a statement by Ronald Ziegler that perfectly mirrored the mood around Mr. Nixon as he approached what his Press Secretary called "that decision point." Ziegler said:

> I am sure the President, based upon these conversations and the conversations that have preceded these and conversations that will follow these, the President will be making decisions. I am sure he has decisions in his mind as to what course he is going to follow on a domestic program. But . . . when you are analyzing anything or discussing anything new, you want to seek all points of view and get all the thinking that there is available before you make a final decision. This is the process that the President is going through.

The process is intended to develop legislative proposals that are more corrective than innovative; to overhaul, partly by amendment of present laws and partly by administrative action, welfare and other social programs that Nixon and his advisers consider to have been hastily and badly conceived and, on the whole, to have failed to deliver anything near all that their beneficiaries were promised and that American society requires. There is a search, made imperative by the overriding need to counter inflation with a big budget surplus in the next fiscal year and curtailed federal expenditures, for remedial measures that will cost as little as possible. A controlling assumption is that no major social legislation can be put through Congress in time to be effective before 1970–71, at the earliest, and in some instances—such as proposals to bring welfare payments up to a minimum and decent national level—before 1972–73. The assumption is probably realistic, but it encourages delay in the name of prayerful study of the options offered the President before he chooses and acts.

Mr. Nixon's insistence that controversial proposals be thoroughly checked out with key legislators of both parties before he commits himself to anything may be nothing more than the "practical politics" that it is claimed to be, but it also makes for delay. Even while telling the press on April 7 that action and plenty of it was near at hand, the President's spokesman took care to say, "I wouldn't want to put a date on anything." The next day, knocking down reports that a revised Model Cities program had been adopted, he emphasized that "there's been no final decision by the President on this or any other program." Only a state of nerves not previously evident at the Nixon White House could explain the botched announcement of a plan to concentrate $200 million-plus of previously appropriated funds upon a belated clean-up and renewal of riot-ruined areas in 20 or more cities. At a press session staged next to Nixon's office, Moynihan persisted in calling it "new money" when it wasn't new and attempted, rather awkwardly, to becloud the patent fact that a portion of the funds had to be diverted from other urban programs in order to make the showing wanted by the President. Nixon's assertion in a written (and garbled) statement that he had "made funds available" compounded the impression of a contrived effort and marred an otherwise laudable move to prod city authorities toward action that, as

the President and Moynihan said, should have been taken months
and, in some places, years ago. The long inaction, they said,
demonstrated "the impotence of modern government at all levels,"
and they intended with this program, sadly mangled though it was
at the start, to dramatize the President's determination to improve
governmental performance "at all levels."

Nixon concluded in early March, after his return from Europe,
that the performance at his own level could stand considerable
improvement. The staff assistance that he was getting on the
domestic side of his affairs seemed to him to be inferior to what
he was getting from his reorganized and enlarged national security
staff through its chief, Henry A. Kissinger. By comparison with
the profusion of ideas, analysis and advice pouring in upon him
from the domestic departments and agencies through the assistants
who were supposed to put it all in order for his perusal, the flow
of foreign-policy paper through Kissinger alone seemed to be
marvelously well arranged. What he needed, the President decided,
was comparable coordination of the domestic flow. He assigned the
task of accomplishing it to John Ehrlichman, a Seattle lawyer who
has done campaign work for him since the 1950's and is the
White House Counsel.

So went the agreed account. One version of it (in an Evans-
Novak column) had it that Ehrlichman had thus been vested with
great influence and that his friend and the President's nominal
Chief of Staff, H. R. "Bob" Haldeman, had lost much face. This
interpretation exaggerated Haldeman's prior role and missed the
point of and reason for Ehrlichman's expanded role. Haldeman,
contrary to the general impression, had always been concerned
more with the form than with the substance of the domestic proposals and recommendations routed through him and his staff to
the President. What Nixon actually missed and sought was a check
that he felt he had not been getting upon the substance—the basic
adequacy—of the domestic policy papers coming to him. He also
felt that the oral explanations and arguments which supplement
the papers could be improved. The important paper still flows
through Haldeman and a staff headed by his young assistant, staff
secretary Kenneth Cole. But it goes now to Ehrlichman and *his*

staff before it finally reaches the President, and Nixon looks to Ehrlichman for assurance that the written material is in sufficient and actionable order.

The assistant chiefly affected by the change is not Haldeman but Arthur Burns, a distinguished economist who alone among the Nixon helpers has Cabinet status. At the time of his appointment as Counsellor in January, he was charged by the President with "the coordination of the development of my domestic policies and programs." He has labored prodigiously, he still has the President's confidence and ready access to Nixon. But the arrangement has not worked as well as Burns and his own assistants seem to think it has. Among his many other chores, Burns has prepared and fired off to various federal agencies more than 100 demands for review of old policies and practices and for new ideas. The inquirer is told by other Presidential assistants, including some who have profound respect for Burns, that the response to these directives has been slow and, in Nixon's view, seriously inadequate. The President has turned to Ehrlichman for more vigorous followups, including when necessary flat orders to the department and agency officials concerned to get off their duffs and answer the Nixon inquiries with satisfactory speed.

Changes and adjustments of this kind occur with every new Presidency and any brief account of them can do injustice to the people involved, the President included. The predominant impression conveyed at the Nixon White House is still that this President is supported by a remarkably amicable group. The senior dozen or so among his assistants have been meeting since early March every morning, Monday through Friday, at 7:45 o'clock, in a staff conference conducted by Haldeman. The purpose is to see to it that everybody working for the President knows what everybody is up to. The inevitable rivalries, the rise or decline of this or that individual in the President's favor, are never evident at these meetings. All is friendly. There are jokes. "I wouldn't have believed that I could laugh at anything at that hour," one of the participants said the other day, "but I do." And he added, staring at his skeptical caller, "It really is fun working here, you know—working for Dick."

The Liberal Republicans

A notion is abroad that the Republicans in Congress are coming down with a severe case of liberalism. The infection is alleged to be especially acute in the Senate. President Nixon's obvious assumption that the national trend is conservative is said to be questioned by an important number of Republican Senators. His barely existent legislative program is reported to be in peril from dissident Republicans and partisan Democrats alike. His loyal and bumbling leader of the Senate minority, Everett M. Dirksen of Illinois, is similarly reported to be in danger of displacement by outraged Republican colleagues.

There is some basis for these impressions, but not as much as recent accounts indicate. It doesn't take much liberalism for a Republican Senator to be labeled a liberal, which is to say, an active or potential rebel against the Nixon-Dirksen leadership. Senate statistics put the matter in its proper perspective. There

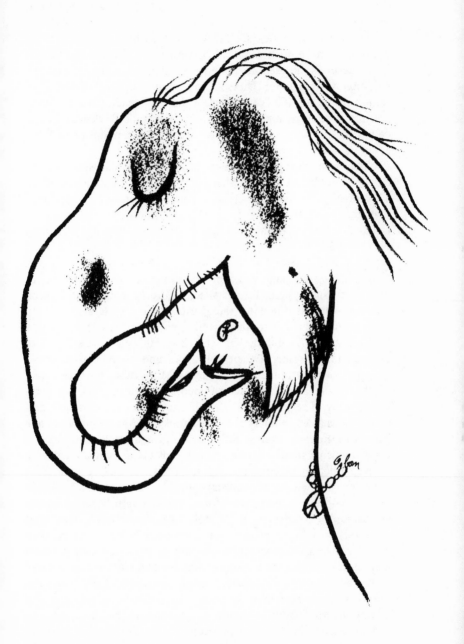

are 43 Republican Senators. The most wishful estimates count
no more than 15 of them as either consistent or occasional liberals
if the term is deemed to connote anything beyond intermittent
irritation with Senator Dirksen and spotty support of Administration proposals. The reputation of the President's party for fiscal
and social caution, and the Nixon Administration's declared dedication to the same, are perfectly safe with the majority of GOP
Senators.

Nobody in Washington is more aware of this than such veteran
Republican liberals as John Sherman Cooper of Kentucky, Clifford
Case of New Jersey, and George Aiken of Vermont. They know
that they and their few fellows are a minority, and a rather
isolated minority at that, within the Senate minority. President
Nixon has done nothing to diminish their isolation. Despite their
seniority and personal prestige, they never gained access to Mr.
Nixon to present their views in opposition to the deployment of
an anti-missile system, for instance, before he committed himself
and his Administration to Safeguard. Senator Case had to wait
three months for a requested meeting with the President and was
finally granted 20 minutes in late June. He and others like him
understand, as some of their colleagues and many journalists do
not, that such current issues as the ABM do more to distort than
to clarify the actual balance of ideologies within their congressional party. The substantial Republican opposition that they and
younger Senators, notably Edward Brooke of Massachusetts, have
been able to rally against Safeguard and against the testing and
deployment of multi-warhead rockets reflects a significant degree
of Republican independence on these issues. But it is a poor
indicator of Senate Republican attitudes toward the kind of
measures—welfare and tax reform, crime control, racial equity
are examples—that separate liberals from conservatives and lend
whatever meaning remains to those tattered terms. Lesser but
also substantial Republican opposition to present levels of military spending, with the accompanying demand for "new priorities"
in the allocation of resources, will be meaningful only when the
time comes to determine the uses to which Congress puts the
money diverted from arms—if useful amounts are diverted.

The impression that Senate Republicans are headed along a
newly enlightened course arises in part from the performances of

five of this year's Republican freshmen and from that of a sixth, Charles E. Goodell of New York, who was appointed by Governor Rockefeller to Robert Kennedy's seat last year. Goodell, William B. Saxbe of Ohio, Charles McC. Mathias of Maryland, Marlow W. Cook of Kentucky, and Richard S. Schweiker of Pennsylvania have defied the tradition that Senate fledglings should be seldom seen or heard and thereby have drawn much attention. Robert Packwood of Oregon, who defeated Wayne Morse and at 36 is the youngest Senator, has ducked attention in the belief, possibly sound, that his calculated modesty and his relatively restrained views will get him farther and faster along the Senate road than the aggressive tactics of his fellow-juniors will get them.

If liberal stances won the general esteem of Republican Senators, Goodell would be their darling. He isn't. He is for rapid disengagement from Vietnam, for cutting military expenditures and increasing social expenditures, for a vigorous attack on hunger, for humane anti-crime measures, against big farm subsidies. He flew to Nigeria to make a case for effective aid to starving Biafrans, to San Francisco to dramatize the case of the Presidio "mutineers," to Los Angeles to lead an anti-ABM rally and to support that city's Negro candidate for mayor, Thomas Bradley. He pledged support for Mayor John Lindsay of New York, regardless of whether he won the Republican nomination, and kept the promise after Lindsay lost to a blatant conservative. Alone among Senators, Goodell took the floor to denounce Dirksen for his autocratic veto, in behalf of the American Medical Association, of Dr. John Knowles' abandoned nomination to be an assistant secretary of HEW. Goodell, whose voting record during four terms in the House prepared nobody for his present behavior, acknowledges that "I have a problem now with instant recognition and with my reputation for instant liberalism." The sad truth is that his Senate colleagues, of all persuasions, will not be as sorry as they should be if he is defeated for nomination and election in 1970.

Senators Saxbe and Cook suffer, though not as greatly, from a comparable reputation for "campaigning one way and voting another." They were grateful to Senator James B. Pearson of Kansas, who is in little or no danger of being called a liberal, for placing in the *Congressional Record* a news story that argued,

with more kindness than accuracy, that their Senate positions are
quite consistent with their campaign positions. They oppose ABM
and multi-rocket deployment, vigorously advocate "new priorities"
and reduced military spending and commitments, and maintain
that the Nixon Administration so far has been much less alive
than it ought to be to "the enormity of the discontent in this
country." They oppose Safeguard on grounds that it will cost too
much, probably won't work, probably will be outmoded even if
it does work, and therefore entails a waste of money. They say,
as Cook puts it, that this shows them to be "true fiscal conservatives" and "consistent conservatives" rather than "liberals." They

promised in their campaigns to oppose extension of the surtax
and declare, in distinctly un-liberal fashion, that no amount of
attached tax reform will persuade them to vote for it.

Mathias and Schweiker came to the Senate from the House,
where they earned reputations which they are sustaining now.
The surtax excepted, they share most of the positions taken and
concerns expressed by Saxbe and Cook, but all four of them say
that a tendency to group them at the core of an emerging liberal
Republican bloc exaggerates the nature and degree of their collaboration. Like Saxbe and Cook, Mathias and Schweiker dis-
courage a similar tendency to identify the most emphatic liberal
of the lot, Charlie Goodell, with them, and their own liberalism
is considerably short of total. Schweiker, for example, talks in

standard conservative style when he applauds President Nixon's preference for "strict constructionists" who will "interpret the Constitution, not rewrite it," on the Supreme Court.

Confronted with the suggestion that he has lain so low as to be almost invisible, Senator Packwood said that "I have, and I am glad that I have." He is for Safeguard, against multi-warhead deployment before arms negotiations are opened with the Russians, for surtax extension ("with some reluctance"), and not discernibly against any major Nixon domestic policy. Yet Senator Aiken, a shrewd judge of his younger compatriots, perceives in Packwood the makings of a valued moderate, if not downright liberal, Republican associate and rates him among the best of the new Senators. However accurate this judgment may prove to be, Bob Packwood is certainly nearer the Republican norm than the more vociferous dissidents are. He was the only Republican freshman invited by Nixon to join 25 congressional establishment types, Republican and Democratic, for a nighttime cruise on the Presidential yacht *Sequoia,* in June.

Have the nonconformist Republicans, whether liberals or "true conservatives" in the Cook-Saxbe mode, had any impact upon Administration policy? "Ask me that 30 days from now and I may be able to answer," Senator Mathias said in late June. Mr. Nixon has made some effort, though not much, to have an impact upon a few of them. He has done Cook and Saxbe the rare honor of inviting them to the White House for private talks lasting an hour or so, mostly about their stands against Safeguard. Some of the others have been included in group occasions, such as the President's Sunday services in the East Room of the White House and the coffee sessions that usually follow. Only once, however, had the President asked a group of Senators identified with the liberal-to-moderate wing of the party down for a serious discussion. That occurred on the late afternoon of June 30, and the event deserved more notice than it got in the national press.

Three of the President's five guests were Schweiker, Cook, and Mathias. The others were Pearson of Kansas and Charles Percy of Illinois, who was invited in the stead of Senator Brooke, who had to bow out because of a death in his family. It appeared afterward to at least some of the Senators that they had experienced Mr. Nixon's major effort to date to counter the developing impression that he was turning—predictably enough, but still disconcertingly for such Senators as Percy and Schweiker—away from them and to the extreme Republican right. The subject uppermost on the President's mind was Vietnam, and his way of appeasement was to tell them what they wanted to hear. From the leaks that the President should have anticipated and probably did, it also appeared that he had scrapped the cautions that had previously hedged his announced policy of disengagement. He proposed, he was said to have said, to withdraw just about all American troops, combat and support, from South Vietnam and he hoped to complete the process before the 1970 congressional elections. This he intended (or hoped?) to do regardless of how the war and the Paris negotiations went. It was a political necessity: Republican candidates for Congress would be sunk in 1970 and he would be sunk in 1972 if it were not accomplished. In forgoing "military victory," as he had in his May 14 Vietnam policy speech, he had also forfeited the option of re-escalating the war. His only practical alternative, and this neither he nor any of his spokesmen had ever said before, was complete military withdrawal rather than the limited withdrawal previously indicated by him and recently advocated, to his seeming irritation, by former Defense Secretary Clark Clifford. Asked to verify or deny a *Los Angeles Times* report based upon the leaked accounts, a White House press spokesman let the story stand.

Whether or not Mr. Nixon said and meant all that he was understood to have said, he had the intended effect upon one of his guests. "I was extremely pleased," Percy later wrote in one of his periodic letters to Illinois Republicans, "by the positive tone of the President's remarks."

X

Laird and Leaks

At the morning meeting of the President's senior staff on April 28, Henry A. Kissinger, the assistant for national security affairs, was asked about the latest of many news reports to the effect that Mr. Nixon has decided to withdraw large numbers of troops from Vietnam this year and intends to do it regardless of what happens in the Paris negotiations and in Vietnam. Kissinger said that the report was not correct. There had been no such decision, there was no such intention. Then where, he was asked, were the persistent rumors to the contrary coming from? "One must assume," Kissinger replied, "that they are coming from the seventh floor of the State Department."

The seventh floor is where Secretary of State William P. Rogers, Under Secretaries Elliott Richardson and U. Alexis Johnson, and the Secretary's *de facto* chief of staff, department Counselor Richard Pedersen, have their offices. When the President was asked at a press conference on April 18 whether he was "considering now the unilateral withdrawal of American troops from South Vietnam," he answered: "I am not. If we are to have a negotiating position at the Paris peace talks, it must be a position in which

Triceratops **Laird**

Osborn

we can negotiate from strength, and discussion about unilateral withdrawal does not help that position." The word was passed that there was to be no official departure whatever from his statement of troop policy at the same conference:

> It is the aim of this Administration to bring men home just as soon as our security will allow us to do so. . . . There are three factors that we are going to take into consideration: the training of the South Vietnamese, their ability to handle their own defense; the level of fighting in South Vietnam, whether or not the offensive action of the enemy recedes; and progress in the Paris peace talks. . . . I think there are good prospects that American forces can be reduced, but . . . we have no plans to reduce our forces until there is more progress on one or all of the three fronts that I have mentioned.

Secretary Rogers stimulated expectations of withdrawal but stayed within the President's guidelines when he said three days later that, "We are not prepared to assume that the only alternative to early progress in the peace talks is an indefinite extension of our present role."

The reports "on high authority" that the President is determined to reduce the forces in Vietnam this year, progress or no progress on his three fronts, continued to appear. Some of them read as if they came from Secretary of Defense Melvin R. Laird, who during his years in Congress and during the Nixon campaign last year was a practiced planter of unattributed items. An inquirer into this possibility at the Pentagon was advised to look instead toward the President's Director of Communications, Herbert Klein. The White House press secretary, Ronald Ziegler, seemed to be more amused than disturbed when he acknowledged at a routine briefing that the President was "aware" of the reports and, the press was allowed to suppose, doing nothing to halt them. Now here was Kissinger, the President's staff adviser on foreign policy and the architect of current Vietnam policy, inviting his fellows at the top of the White House establishment to "assume" that the reports originated in the vicinity of Mr. Nixon's dear friend and long-time associate, the Secretary of State. Kissinger himself firmly refused to go beyond the public position in off-record conversations and was said to believe that the reports that he attributed to "the seventh floor" had diminished what chance there may have been to persuade the Hanoi representatives in Paris to negotiate a mutual withdrawal of American and North Vietnamese forces.

A student of the Administration suggested to two White House officials, one of high rank and one of middle rank, that these goings-on reflected either a rather transparent job of managed propaganda, aimed at pacifying opponents of the war, or a state of condoned disorder behind the facade of Nixon order. The ranking official smiled and said nothing. The junior official grimaced: "Let us hope that it is the former." His tone indicated a suspicion that it is the latter.

There certainly is more disorder behind the facade than the early show of Nixon efficiency indicated. Henry Kissinger's expanded national security operation, for instance, is hardly the model of efficiency that the President, among others, has imagined it to be. The section heads of Kissinger's staff, men of some distinction in their various fields, rarely see him except at National Security Council meetings dealing with their subjects. Kissinger has refused so far to appoint a deputy with overall authority, and he himself is so burdened with the President's demands and with Council business that he has no time for orderly management of the staff. The backlog of unattended policy paper on his desk is always enormous. He goes at it by fits and starts, and tries to make up for the delays by demanding responses to his inquiries, from his own staff and from the Department of State, within what the victims consider to be impossibly short time limits. There is no evidence that all of this has affected the quality of Kissinger's service to the President, which is what matters, but it contrasts oddly with the image of cool proficiency that the Nixon White House tries to project.

For an example of serious botchery, let us turn to the ABM issue and the Administration's management of it. Behind his appearance of aggressive confidence, there is no sadder figure in Washington than Defense Secretary Laird. He is said at the Pentagon to sense that he somehow failed, in his televised testimony before the Senate Armed Services and Foreign Relations committees, to put himself and the Safeguard system he was defending across as he intended to do. He said at one point that he wanted more than anything else to be remembered as "the Secretary of

Peace," and at another that his mother had told him after one of his appearances that the average viewer would be expecting the world to go up in nuclear dust. How is it, he keeps asking his intimates, that his talk about giant Soviet SS-9 rockets and the Soviet's aiming for a "first-strike capability" could have been so misunderstood? Cartoons suggesting that he hungers for holocaust are said to pain him deeply. Was he not, as a Congressman, known as "Mr. Health" because of his long and effective advocacy of large appropriations for health care and research? Surely, he says in private, sensible citizens cannot fail to realize that he would much rather be devoting the billions now going for defense to the nation's social needs. He must have done something wrong, he acknowledges, but he cannot for the life of him figure what it was.

The President, watching the opposition to Safeguard mount in the Senate and in the country, should be able to figure it out if he puts his mind to it. All he has to do is remember certain episodes in the 1968 campaign. Congressman Laird accompanied the candidate as his official hatchet-man, saying the rude things and dropping hints of Democratic perfidy that were thought to be too crass for Mr. Nixon. On at least two occasions, Congressman Laird overspoke himself and Nixon had to explain away, as best he could, the resultant messes. Just why, after this experience, President Nixon placed Melvin Laird at the head of the Defense Department is a puzzle that becomes more interesting by the day.

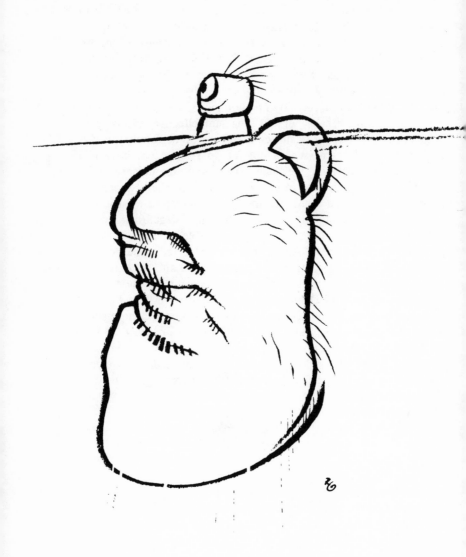

The Rise of Harry Dent

Whatever it was that happened at the White House and changed his life and the lives of several other people in late April, Harry Dent says, it happened while he was abroad and he didn't have a thing to do with it. All that Harry admits to knowing about it is what other people, including the President, told him when Harry got back from a trip to Europe and Asia with Secretary of Commerce Maurice Stans. Harry isn't saying what they told him, except that from then on he was to be recognized and respected by everybody at the White House and by everybody concerned with the affairs of the Republican party as the President's personally chosen and empowered "political coordinator."

The news was slow in getting out, presumably because neither the President nor Harry Dent nor anyone else at the White House was anxious to have it known. When it did leak out, it was of more than passing interest because of Harry's background. He is known in Washington and throughout the sub-world of national politics as Senator Strom Thurmond's man. Aged 39, a lawyer, a native of South Carolina and still a deacon and trustee of the Kathwood Baptist Church in Columbia, the state capital and his family home, he worked for Senator Thurmond from January 1, 1955, until his appointment to the incoming White House staff was announced last December. It was one of the first Nixon appointments, it occurred after Senator Thurmond conferred with the President-elect in New York, and it was announced with more fanfare than the choice of a deputy assistant to the President usually receives. Dent acknowledges that the appointment was made in recognition of Senator Thurmond's services to Nixon in holding decisive portions of the South for him at the nominating convention and afterward.

Now Dent himself, the entire White House establishment, and the Nixon leadership recently installed at the Republican National Committee headquarters in Washington are engaged in promoting a new identity for Harry. The way the press keeps pinning the Thurmond tag on Harry Dent is said to be a sin and a shame, a bitter injustice to a brilliant master of practical politics. The sanctioned word is that Harry Dent is no longer Strom Thurmond's man. He is Richard Nixon's man. Dent prefers to do his part in fashioning the new identity on an off-record basis, but he allows himself to be quoted as follows:

> Senator Thurmond is certainly a good friend of mine, and I feel that he is a good friend of this Administration. The Senator has always known that this Administration could not agree with all of the Thurmond positions. He very clearly understands that I am working for Richard Nixon and that my loyalty is to Richard Nixon. Senator Thurmond demands and expects your complete loyalty when you are working for him, and he expects that you will give the same loyalty to anybody else you are working for.

Nixon is said to have asked and received firm assurances to the same effect from Thurmond before Dent was appointed. Through Jack Ravan, one of his assistants, Senator Thurmond was invited to state his understanding of his present personal and working relationship, if any, with Dent. Ravan consulted the Senator and said that he wished to be quoted as follows: "Mr. Harry Dent is a man of splendid character and ability. He brings to the job a man dedicated to constitutional government."

John Sears, a 28-year-old lawyer who was thought until lately to be doing a good job for Mr. Nixon as his political coordinator, shares Suite 166 in the Executive Office Building, next door to the White House, with Harry Dent and might be supposed to know why he was summarily displaced after three years of close association with the President. Sears was a junior employe of the former Nixon law firm in New York when he was transferred to Nixon's personal staff in early 1966. He has no political ties to anybody except the President. His skill at sizing up politicians and political situations is attested by men who worked with him for Nixon's nomination and election, and he is given much of the credit for keeping Vice President Agnew from becoming more of a liability than he was during the 1968 campaign. Why, then, the President's decision in April to supersede him with Harry Dent?

When Sears proved to be discreetly vague on the subject, I told him (for needling purposes) that I had observed to a couple of his admirers on the White House staff that it looked to me as if he had been the victim of "a plain, old-fashioned nut-cutting operation." Suppositions and remarks of this kind are not appreciated at the Nixon White House and I half expected Sears to throw me out of his office. He didn't. With a look of amused and detached interest on his owlish face, he wanted to know what his friends had said. When he was told that they had accepted the suggestion in silence, Sears indicated that he couldn't care less. Rumors that he was about to quit were false. He was staying as a deputy assistant, on the staff of Counsel John Ehrlichman, which also is Dent's official status and title. At the request and with the blessing of the President, Sears would be planning over the long range and thinking about how to win Republican victories in 1970 and 1972 and—one gathered—happily leaving the grubby details of day-to-day political coordination to Harry Dent.

Political coordination is a euphemism for what Congressman Rogers C. B. Morton of Maryland, who was chosen by Nixon to be chairman of the Republican National Committee, calls the "nitty-gritty type of detail that has to be interacted between the

White House and the National Committee." Getting big-money con-
tributors invited to White House dinners and receptions is an
example of nitty-gritty. Making sure that good Republicans are
preferred for appointive jobs is another example. Giving Republicans who work at being Republicans, in Congress and elsewhere,
a sense that they have at the White House a friend who will answer
the telephone when they call, whose values are their values, is the
supreme essence of nitty-gritty. Richard Nixon, a nitty-gritty politician if there ever was one, did not permit these aspects of the
Presidency and of his party responsibilities to be altogether neglected during his first months in the office. But, outwardly and to
some extent in fact, he tried to place himself above and away from
them. Morton's predecessor at the National Committee, Ray Bliss,
and the Committee as such had practically no communication with
the Nixon White House and were almost wholly excluded from
the early patronage process. John Sears, with his clinically intelligent approach to politics and politicians, and two other Presidential assistants dealing with personnel matters, Harry Flemming
and Peter Flanigan, simply did not strike orthodox Republicans
as the proper types to be vetting candidates for high-level, high-
pay appointments before they were approved and announced by
the President. It was not so much that Nixon's talent hunters
scorned Republican applicants—they didn't; far from it—but that
they looked first for good *Nixon* Republicans, second for good
party men, and that they actually seemed to believe all that Nixon
stuff about quality first and party next. Before he accepted the
Committee chairmanship, Rogers Morton came to an understanding with Nixon that this sort of nonsense would have to be curbed,
and that essentially is why Harry Dent replaced John Sears as the
President's man at the nitty-gritty level of White House politics.

Watching Harry Dent at work is a joy. In contrast with the
tanned, lean, tailored chaps from advertising and the law who
dominate Nixon's immediate staff, Harry is a slightly pudgy man
who appears to regard clothing as a necessary nuisance. His low-
country South Carolina accent, unimpaired by his years in Washington, lends an extra dimension to the political business he trans-
acts by telephone from eight in the morning until midnight and

later. A recent nighttime caller who could not avoid overhearing snatches of a conversation (at 9 p.m.) with Secretary of Labor George Shultz was entranced by the way Harry murmured: "Now, I'll tell you, Mister Seckerterry," and proceeded to tell. Harry would never tell a Cabinet Secretary what to do or not to do. But he is free to suggest that in a delicate matter the Secretary let so-and-so have his say, or consult a state chairman or a generous businessman or a powerful labor leader, just making certain that all the bases are touched before something is done that might make trouble for "the man in the Oval Office." Robert Brown, a former public relations man from North Carolina and Nixon's ranking black assistant, is one of the many who speak well of Harry Dent. Harry has what it takes for his job, Bob Brown says, and never mind certain differences of view that a white Southerner and a black Southerner are born with. And, Brown joins the White House chorus in saying, never mind Harry's past ties.

The Dent assignment is one of several ways in which Nixon is tying his Presidency closer to the Republican party and its needs. Rogers Morton, discussing these moves at a recent press conference, made it clear that he is going to look for a lot of cooperation from, among others on the Nixon staff, Communications Director Herbert Klein. The National Committee staff is getting geared to give Nixon speeches, statements and other official White House material a distribution for political purposes that the executive office could not legally finance. The Cabinet Secretaries have been told to designate staffers who will be at the National Committee's disposal as Dent and Klein are at the White House. What Morton has requested and been promised at each department and agency is "a sort of political pivot, [a] person that we can talk to who has the ear of the Secretary or Director [so that] we do have an opportunity to at least review and advise in matters of appointment." Although nobody says so, Harry Dent is to be the director and overseer of this entire politicizing process—not exaggerating the importance of party politics in the Presidential picture, he insists, but merely according it the place in the scheme it should have had all along.

Dent's credentials for the assignment are impeccable. What seems grubby and dull to men like Sears, Flemming, and Flanigan

seems to Harry Dent to be sensible, exciting, and downright good.
He was a Democrat, standard Southern and South Carolina style,
until Strom Thurmond switched to the Republicans and Goldwater in 1964, when Harry did, too. Thurmond sent him home to
South Carolina in late 1965, to take over the state party and
organize it for Thurmond's reelection as a Republican in 1966.
Dent figured, coldly and factually, that to win Strom had to run
as the white man's candidate (as he had always run, for that
matter), and that with his past record of nigger-baiting he had no
chance of attracting black votes. So Harry shaped the South
Carolina Republican stance accordingly—not just to get Thurmond reelected, he says now, but to establish a permanent and
effective Republican second party in one-party South Carolina.
Twenty-five Republicans were elected to the state assembly, a
surprising number of others won locally, and Dent didn't argue
with people who said he was a miracle worker. In 1968, when as
state chairman and Thurmond's man he ran the Nixon campaign
in South Carolina and four other Southeastern states, his South
Carolina Republicans took a terrible beating in their home races,
but South Carolina and three others of Dent's five states went for
Nixon. Dent and Thurmond aimed their campaign for Nixon at
George Wallace rather than at Hubert Humphrey, and as things
turned out Nixon would have lacked an electoral majority if the
tactic had failed and Wallace had won in what Dent now calls
his states. For this, and for Dent's work at the Miami Beach convention to blunt Governor Ronald Reagan's great appeal to South
Carolina and other Southern delegates, Nixon was duly grateful.
He is said to have made something of a study of Harry Dent after
the election, and to have concluded that he is in fact as skilled
at political nitty-gritty as his admirers (Harry included) say he is.

   In his first months at the White House, Dent behaved pretty
much as Thurmond's man was expected to. He had a hand in
postponing showdowns with several segregated Southern school
districts, including two in South Carolina, but abandoned them to
their fate once it became clear that they had been foolish enough
to believe the explicit assurances of Strom Thurmond and the implied promises of Richard Nixon that they would not have to in-
tegrate if Nixon was elected. Dent also intervened in behalf of
three Southern textile firms that were about to lose military cloth-

ing contracts because they had failed to hire Negroes in the proportions required by law and defense regulations. It was Deputy
Defense Secretary David Packard, not Dent, who waived the written guarantees required by law and settled for oral assurances from
the firms, and one is asked at the White House to believe that
Dent had nothing to do with the latter phases of the case. His trip
to Europe and the Far East with Commerce Secretary Stans was
arranged in order to show Southern textile, tobacco, and soybean
producers that the Nixon Administration is as eager as it claims
it is to protect their markets at home and abroad from hurtful
competition. The Stans mission appears to have been a roaring
failure, but nobody blames Harry for that and the affected producers are assumed to be grateful to Nixon for sending their friend
along.

The word is that Dent's Southern and parochial concerns are
over with. The scope of his services to and for President Nixon
is intended to be national from now on out. Rogers Morton and
his reorganized staff at the National Committee are tickled pink
and there is no better authority on what is expected of Harry, in
his role as Richard Nixon's man than the new Republican chairman. Quoting Morton:

> We will develop with Harry a working relationship that will provide
> the President through him a good briefing of what we're doing, of
> what the political situation is . . . It simplifies the thing a great deal
> if we've got somebody that we can call and get to quickly and they
> have got somebody that has the time to call our committee and get
> information quickly . . . We also would expect from Harry a lot of
> advice and counsel and what the interpretations of the White House
> are in connection with political strategy and situations. I believe that
> Harry is a very knowledgeable person and he's got a lot of energy
> and we will probably work his office pretty hard.

That's for sure and Harry will love it.

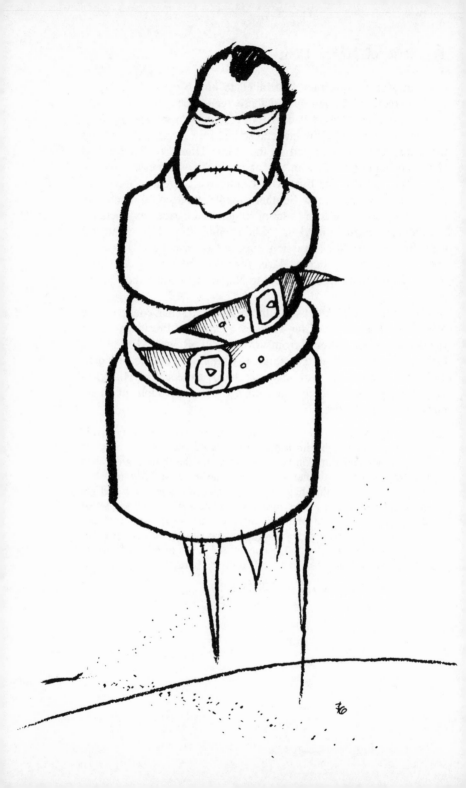

XII

Bouncing Back

The study of Richard Nixon, an exercise to which I have devoted most of my time since September of 1968, requires a steadfast clinging to the fact that he is human. That is not easy. Most of the people who work for him at the White House do their witless best to conceal the fact, making him out to be a President who never—but *never*—succumbs to the pressures of the office and who in all other conceivable ways is without fault or foible. For example, I set out in June to test the supposition that the Presidency must have worked some changes in Mr. Nixon, in his approach to the job and in his ways of dealing with it and with those who help him in it. The answer I got, with an exception to be noted below, was that the Presidency has had no discernible and material effect of any kind upon Mr. Nixon. He may be a bit more assured, "more formidable" as one of his assistants put it. But in his calm mastery of himself and of his job, in his capacity for deliberate order, in his refusal to be ruffled by the criticism and mishaps that so far have come his way, he is said to be unchanged in any substantial respect from the man who called his first Cabinet meeting to order on January 21.

The exception proves the point of this brief analysis of Mr.

Nixon as he has revealed himself in two recent episodes. I was told, and was astonished at being told within the disciplined precincts of the Nixon White House, that the President fell, some weeks ago, into a passing phase of extreme frustration. "Depression," it was said, would be too strong a word for the mood that he then exhibited. But it was enough to trouble and temporarily dismay the few assistants who observed it. The domestic (not foreign) problems of the economy, of the cities, of the campuses, the actual and latent turmoil at home, seemed for a time to have over-whelmed Mr. Nixon and to have robbed him of his habitual confidence that any problem that has to be solved can be solved. The responses of the major departments and agencies to his early demands for recommended solutions, and the ideas presented to him by his own assistants suddenly seemed to him to be impossibly inadequate. They induced a feeling, not that the people concerned were inadequate, but that the problems themselves were beyond real solution. It was at about this time that the President's habit of withdrawal for hours of lone cogitation began to be emphasized in the press. It was at this time, too, that he had to announce that some of his early promises of a new poverty program, a new welfare policy and the like had been premature and that they would take more time than he had thought they would. But there was no hint, public or private, that the difficulties suggested by these and similar admissions had affected the President himself. For the most part, there still isn't. Instead there is denial that Mr. Nixon went through and has now emerged from any such phase. I am convinced that he did, and that in the soothful atmosphere of the Nixon White House most of the people who surround him never noticed it.

The point is simply that President Nixon is not—he couldn't be—the inhumanly calm and implacably ordered figure that his entourage not only depicts but seems actually to believe him to be. For what used to be called "the real Nixon," the man in the Presidency, the observer must look beyond the people around him to the man himself and to the glimpses of the true Nixon self that he occasionally provides. This he did, it seems to me, in his speech at the Air Force Academy in Colorado Springs on June 4, in his sixth press conference in Washington on June 19, and in his known behavior before and after both those events.

The Colorado speech was the one in which, in the course of a presentable argument for maintaining "the American role in the world" and the military strength associated with it, Mr. Nixon let himself go with a sneer at "the so-called best circles in America" and with the inclusive suggestion that critics of his conception of the role are "new isolationists" who consider "patriotism . . . to be a backward fetish of the uneducated and the unsophisticated." He gave himself and his targets an out: he didn't mean *all* of the critics, naming none. Here, in these parts of the speech, was Nixon at his familiar but recently obscured worst. Here, too, was Nixon precisely as he intended to present himself. He had rehearsed the essence of the speech at a Cabinet meeting, to unanimous applause, and had tried out hunks of it in informal and unnoticed remarks on Armed Forces Day. His staff testified that it was "pure Nixon," originally framed by him and finally revised and polished by him on the night before he delivered it. Afterward, during a two-day interlude in California before he went to Midway Island, he was in unusually high spirits. He was pleased with the speech, with the reaction to it, and with himself. He refused to join his assistants in their anxious postmortems, indicating to them that they were wasting their time and asking him to waste his on idle concern for the adverse reaction that some of them expected.

The June 19 press conference was the occasion for a performance that the press generally took to constitute his first serious blunder and, what was worse, a blunder committed in pique at former Secretary of Defense Clark Clifford. In a magazine article quoted in the newspapers that morning, Clifford had topped Nixon's Midway announcement of the beginning of troop withdrawals from Vietnam with the suggestion that the President commit himself to pulling out some 100,000 men in 1969 and to completing the withdrawal of all ground combat troops by the end of 1970. Mr. Nixon let himself go again, sneering that Clifford in office "did not move" to accomplish what he now proposed and twice venting a hope that this Administration would "beat Mr. Clifford's time table." It was a nasty and, on its face, intemperate reaction that could, as subordinate spokesmen seemed to feel afterward, impair the Paris negotiations. The point of interest here is that Mr. Nixon never spent a calmer day than the one that preceded his evening press conference. He knew of the Clifford article

well before the news of it appeared that morning. He passed the day alone in his Lincoln Study at the Presidential Mansion, consulting others by telephone about what he might be asked and what he should say that night, poring over a few staff memos on the same subject, but in the main preparing himself without assistance. Afterward, he darted off to the last innings of a local ball game. The next morning, obviously exhilarated, he took his Irish setter for an unusual walk through the White House grounds and offices, popped in on a staff meeting where he was observed to be "in a wonderful mood," and through the subsequent days showed not the slightest concern for the widespread judgment that he had, as Senator Mansfield put it, momentarily and perhaps harmfully "blown his cool."

A reasonable conclusion to be drawn is that Nixon, like other men, needs to be himself from time to time. Not the whole self, of course, but the meaner self that he has been in the past and will be again, in the Presidency. I suggest that it's a form of therapy, good for him if not always good for the country.

The Image of Nixon isn't entirely clear!

XIII

Know
Your President

A group of White House reporters had a rare and startling experience the other day. They heard one of the President's principal assistants say something meaningful about Richard Nixon as a person. "He is the kind of fellow," the assistant said, "who has a plan, who knows what he wants to do, and says to himself, 'If everybody will just keep quiet and leave me alone, I'll get it done and everything will be all right.'" The insight was interesting. But the really interesting thing about it was not what was said but that it was said. The Nixonologists of the press are reduced, most of the time, to applying to their study of the President the processes of deductive guessing that Kremlinologists and students of the Hanoi and Peking hierarchies have to rely upon. Here, for once, was a departure from the rule of reticence that Mr. Nixon appears to have imposed upon everybody who works for and associates with him in an official capacity. I say, "appears," because

I don't *know* that Mr. Nixon has imposed such a rule. I deduce that he has from the fact that the people who work for him usually either evade or flatly refuse to answer any question that has to do with his personal behavior and reactions when he is out of public sight.

A notable exception to this pattern of non-response lends itself to endless deduction. Mr. Nixon's people are pleased to say, at every opportunity, that he "enjoys the job" and "gets a bang" out of being President. They imply that his enjoyment, the bang he gets, increases in direct ratio to his troubles. The Nixonologist is invited to deduce, but of course doesn't, that the President chortles every time another Senator announces his intention to vote against the confirmation of Judge Haynsworth's nomination to the Supreme Court, and that the October 15 Vietnam Moratorium positively enraptured Mr. Nixon. What I deduce is a determination at the White House, carried to a point close to desperation in times of stress, to preserve the desired image of a President in unshakable command of his job and the country.

One may deduce from a known fact that Mr. Nixon suspects that something is wrong with the image his servitors are projecting, mostly by trying not to project any personalized image at all. The known fact is that John Ehrlichman, the White House Counsel, has recently added to his expanding responsibilities a review of White House public relations. Is Press Secretary Ronald Ziegler serving the President's best interests with his technique of genial caution and with his studied refusal to flesh out the aseptically sparse account of White House doings that he offers daily? Is Herbert Klein, the President's Director of Communications for the Executive Branch, providing the in-depth background that reporters were led to expect from him when the informational function was divided between him and Ziegler? The short answer to both questions is no. But Ehrlichman may conclude, if he hasn't already, that Messrs. Ziegler and Klein are performing precisely as the President has told them to and that, in this limited sense, they in their careful ways are useful reflectors of Mr. Nixon. If what the President wants and requires is an essentially false reflection of himself, that is worth knowing.

The perils of tinkering with the informational procedures devised for and approved by Nixon when he was the President-elect are illustrated by one of the innovations being considered at the White House. It is to release, either regularly to the entire press or intermittently to favored reporters and pundits, a "sanitized" version of the President's actual schedule on theoretically typical days, rather than the skeletal schedule that is routinely announced. Reporters being the captious creatures they are, the result is foreseeable if this is done. Nobody will believe that the inflated version has been "sanitized" only to protect the national security. The Presidential cosmeticians will be said to have achieved another dubious triumph.

The trouble with the effort to protect the President from candid disclosure of any kind is that it is bound to fail. Chinks open up, with unflattering consequences. There was, for instance, the aftermath of the 50 minutes that Lieut. General Lewis B. Hershey, the nation's draft director since 1941, spent with the President on October 10. Much was made afterward of the reluctance of the White House spokesmen to acknowledge that General Hershey was being relieved in order to dampen the Vietnam protest coming up on October 15. A more interesting disclosure, in the glimpse it gave of Mr. Nixon, came from General Hershey when he said through his own press office that in their time together at the White House "the President did not at any time come right out and say to me, 'You are no longer Director of Selective Service.' "

For days after Marshal Ky of South Vietnam blew the whistle, somewhat inaccurately, on the President's plans for his second increment of troop withdrawals from Vietnam, White House reporters were told that Nixon was not at all perturbed. It was possible to infer from the official account that the episode had been prearranged for trial purposes. In the company of a group that happened to include a young woman, one of the President's closest associates said much later that he would be happy to narrate Nixon's real reaction "if the lady left the room." A trivial thing, it may be argued, but it was typical of the episodes that continually reduce Mr. Nixon's credibility.

The disclosures that do come the assiduous reporter's way create an impression that, more often than not, would be to the President's benefit if it were not in such sharp contrast with the contrived image. An example is the forethought on the part of some members of the Nixon staff that preceded his four weeks of working vacation in California in August and September. Did the President, a restless man, really want to spend that long a time away from Washington? What mix of work and play would suffice to hold him still for an interlude that the concerned staff members thought he genuinely needed? To the relief and considerable surprise of the assistants in question—principally Robert Haldeman, John Ehrlichman, and Dwight Chapin—the President throve upon the mix of work in the mornings and rather stolid play in the afternoons that they arranged for him. I found it interesting, and not at all discreditable to Mr. Nixon, that he was thought to require and appeared to welcome that degree of management by his assistants. But I tend to reflect upon it when I am asked to believe that he is the totally sufficient manager of himself and the country that he is depicted to be.

I have reported that the senior assistants to Henry A. Kissinger, the President's chief staff adviser on foreign policy, "never see the President and never communicate directly with him." That was not a deduction but, up to October 2, a fact of the kind from which I and others around the White House deduced that Mr. Nixon isolates himself to an extraordinary and increasing extent from all except a very few chosen advisers within his own official family. It turns out that on October 2 the President invited Kissinger and his hitherto avoided senior assistants to the White House Cabinet Room for a prolonged, leisurely, and productive talk-fest. It was an unprecedented occasion, not likely to be repeated in the near future. Mr. Nixon may be expected to continue to look to Kissinger, and to Kissinger alone, for the personal delivery of staff advice on foreign policy. The point of mentioning the departure from custom here is that the Nixonologist comes upon happenings of this kind only by accident at the Nixon White House. Instead of cooking up such phoney concessions to reportorial hunger as the sanitized appointments list, the President's managing assistants and his press spokesmen would do better to lower the screen a bit and let the man behind it appear, warts and all, more often than they have done up to now. But that, of course, would require a change in concept and instructions that can come only from the hidden President, and probably never will.

XIV

Who's Who

Nine months after he took office, President Nixon is still fiddling with the staff system at the White House. His senior assistants say that he is not entirely happy with either it or them and add, in a tone of praise rather than complaint, that he probably never will be. They say that it is a mistake to suppose, as I did when I began this inquiry, that the Nixon staff, domestic and foreign, would have settled by now into functional patterns that suit the President and that may be expected to prevail at least through his present term. Behind the show of bland calm and order that Mr. Nixon has imposed upon himself and upon his White House establishment, his assistants acknowledge when they make a virtue of the continuing flux that they are serving a restless, rather uncertain, and chronically dissatisfied man. Some of them also acknowledge that, if the system as it has evolved to date is judged by some of the results, the President ought to be even more dissatisfied than he is said to be.

The "staff system" dealt with here consists of some 50 Presidential appointees and about 100 others who assist the appointees. It is by far the largest and most elaborate personal staff ever as-

sembled by a President to serve his immediate needs. At its top
and core, closest to the President and in frequent—often daily,
sometimes hourly—contact with him are a dozen or so senior
assistants, and it is with a key few among them that this report
is principally concerned. Any outsider who knew all there is to
know—I don't pretend to—about what H. R. (Bob) Haldeman,
John D. Ehrlichman, and Henry A. Kissinger do and are expected
to do for their President would have an understanding of the Nixon
Presidency that actually won't be available until the memoirs of
this Administration appear.

Haldeman, a full assistant who is best described as the President's chief of staff, and Ehrlichman, the White House Counsel,
are the keepers at the Nixon gate. Nobody reaches the President
in person or by telephone, no piece of paper gets to his desk without the knowledge and assent of one or both of them. That is true
even when the President himself initiates a visit or calls for a
paper: he does it through one of them, usually Haldeman, and
he frequently asks one or the other or both of them whether he
should do it. This applies, in Haldeman's case, even to the flow
of paper from Henry Kissinger, the otherwise independent and
self-sufficient foreign policy adviser, and from his National Security
Council staff. If Haldeman thinks a Kissinger paper or Kissinger
view could stand amendment and improvement, he is free to say
so either to Nixon or to Kissinger and occasionally does.

This fact is indicative of a change in the Nixon process that has
occurred so subtly and gradually since the Inauguration in January that other assistants, including some of the seniors, are hardly
aware of it. Mr. Nixon seems to have meant it when he said at the
start that he wanted "all of the options . . . all of the alternatives"
—with emphasis upon *all*—in every area of policy to reach him
undiluted by intermediate selection and judgment. It was an impossible and impractical aim, and the President has recognized
that it was by looking to Ehrlichman and Haldeman on the domestic side, and to Kissinger on the foreign side, for preliminary value
judgments that in intended effect weed out much that in their
opinion would uselessly consume Nixon's time and energy. Ehrlichman is the principal domestic winnower—Haldeman's role is still
basically that of the President's chief dispatcher and manager—
but both of them are, in their evolving functions, assistants with

great and growing power. The sort of men they are, the qualities that presumably lead the President to rely upon them to the extent he does, should tell a good deal about the Nixon Presidency as it is seen from the inside. Here, then, is a foreshortened view of Robert Haldeman and John Ehrlichman as some of their White House associates see and characterize them.

"Pragmatist" is the word applied most often to both of them—to Haldeman, the ex-advertising man and promoter, and to Ehrlichman, the lawyer. The central meaning of the term, not unkindly intended, is that they are more concerned with what will work than with what is right. Haldeman is considered to have the sharper mind, Ehrlichman the broader intellect and the broader range of concerns and interests. Haldeman is valued by other staffers, senior and junior, for what seems to them to be his intimate knowledge and understanding of the President—of what Nixon wants in the way of submitted ideas and of response to his own demands and ideas. His facility in this respect is so esteemed that other assistants, particularly at the secondary level, who in the early months expected direct communication with the President, on paper if not in person, now settle for communication with and from Haldeman on the President's behalf—so long, that is, as they are not totally excluded from the Oval Office. Ehrlichman in his widening policy role is the designated evaluator and compromiser of opposing domestic views, the assistant who more than any other serves the purpose originally assigned to and never quite fulfilled by Counsellor (and Cabinet member) Arthur Burns. Burns, it is worth noting, has a stern sense of what is right in his conservative judgment, and my guess is that his refusal to suppress that sense of rightness has had more than a little to do with his unadmitted but obvious relegation to the policy sidelines. Nixon probably will never grant to Ehrlichman, and Ehrlichman would never claim for himself, the status of a "Deputy President" for domestic matters. But it is acknowledged at the White House that his role is "evolving in that direction" and is already closer to it than many of his staff associates either realize or, in a natural desire to maximize their own positions, care to admit even to themselves.

Nobody at the White House is either reticent or in doubt about Henry Kissinger's role. As of now and until further notice, he is the one indispensable man on the Nixon staff. His policy views aside—and here, it should be manifest, we are more concerned with the mechanics than with the substance of the Nixon operation —it seems true to say and it in fact is said at the White House that Nixon literally could not function without Henry Kissinger at his beck. And that, exaggeration or not, raises the only question really worth raising about the Nixon-Kissinger relationship. It is a question that has to do, in a most serious way, with the President's judgment and with Kissinger's judgment. The question is—what happens, to the President and to the Presidential policy process, if Kissinger all of a sudden isn't there any more? Kissinger would say, and for all I know the President also would say, that it is an absurd question, of a piece with what is regarded in their vicinity as a misguided tendency to magnify the Kissinger role beyond all reality and to denigrate Nixon's own capacity to make and execute foreign policy. But the question is not absurd, it is raised very seriously within the White House counsels, and it does not exaggerate Henry Kissinger's present importance.

It arises primarily from the President's insistence that, within his own establishment, he deal only with Kissinger on foreign-policy matters. The Cabinet-level National Security Council serves as a revived and valued forum for group discussion. Kissinger has his own secretariat and associated NSC staff, enlarged and elaborated beyond all previous practice. But Nixon does not want Kissinger to have, and Kissinger does not want to have, any subordinate who comes anywhere near to being an effective deputy to the Assistant for National Security Affairs. Kissinger is the only Presidential appointee on the extensive Kissinger-NSC staff (the only other such appointee, Richard V. Allen, who directed Nixon's foreign policy research during the 1968 campaign, resigned after nine months of utter isolation from both Nixon and Kissinger). Kissinger presides over and dominates the interdepartmental "review group" that screens policy communications from State, Defense, and CIA to the President. Everything prepared for the President by Kissinger's prolific staff goes to Nixon in Kissinger's name. Occasional attendance at NSC sessions aside, his senior assistants never see the President and never communicate directly with him. Until recently, they enjoyed a minimum of direct access to and communication with Kissinger himself. Here again, the chief cause was not arrogance but the President's preferred way of work and the heavy demands he placed and still places upon Kissinger's time.

Kissinger, brought to recognize the defect, has lately undertaken to have at least two staff meetings each week, with his senior assistants. Some weeks he manages it, some weeks he doesn't. Several of his assistants, senior and junior, have left his service and some others probably will. In every case, there have been explanations other than disaffection or ideological differences with Kissinger. But his shop has come to be known throughout government as a tough place to work and Henry Kissinger as a hard man to work for and satisfy. That may be to his credit— I think it is. His staff arrangements for better policy thought and planning than he considers he gets from State, and for in-depth "program analysis" of a kind intended to meld in one package all of the factors bearing upon major foreign commitments, promise substantial improvement in the advisory process. But the facts behind the reputation do not fit the picture of a smooth and flawless foreign-policy operation that the White House spokesmen try to purvey.

Discussing Kissinger, his White House operation and his relationship with Nixon without bringing up Secretary of State William P. Rogers and *his* relationships with Nixon and Kissinger would be a breach of journalistic custom. Here I summarize what I believe to be Henry Kissinger's view of the matter. He is at least as fed up with the incessant discussion of it as Rogers is. He understands that Rogers, thanks to his friendship of more than 20 years with Richard Nixon, has a relationship and standing with the President that Henry Kissinger doesn't have and probably never will have. He also understands that if he were ever foolish enough to let the undeniable tension between him and Rogers, and between Kissinger's staff and Rogers' State Department, degenerate into a knockdown, cut-throat fight for the President's favor and esteem, William Rogers would almost certainly emerge the winner. Kissinger was not present, and a fair guess is that he did not expect or ask to be present, when Nixon and Rogers spent 90 minutes together on a Monday in October and scheduled another long and private session together on the following Wednesday, ranging over foreign policy from Vietnam to the Middle East. Rogers has yet to claim or establish effective command over his own department. But nobody who knows him and has any conception of his hold upon Nixon's affection and respect could believe that he is in less than adequate command of the Kissinger-Nixon-Rogers situation.

XV

Struggle for Neatness

A few days after a reorganization of the White House staff was announced on November 4, I remarked to one of the assistants who was affected by it that an event of this kind has meaning for most people only in the sense and to the extent that it tells something about Mr. Nixon. What, if anything, did this one signify in terms of the President—his approach to policy, his view of his job? The assistant thought the question over and replied as follows:

> Policy? It doesn't mean a thing in terms of policy. Sure, Pat Moynihan is a liberal Democrat, the only one around here, and he goes up. Arthur Burns is a conservative, and he's going out (if you can say that becoming chairman of the Federal Reserve Board is "going out"). But Bryce Harlow and John Ehrlichman are conservative types, and they are going up. If I had to read a meaning into this, I guess I'd say that it's the biggest thing that's happened so far in the President's continuing struggle for neatness.

The staff changes were aimed at bringing to the formulation and execution of domestic policy the sort of neatness that Henry A. Kissinger, the President's assistant for national security affairs, appears to Mr. Nixon to have achieved on the foreign policy side. The man chosen to accomplish this improbable domestic miracle is John D. Ehrlichman, hitherto White House Counsel and now Assistant to the President for Domestic Affairs. The White House announcement said that he "will advise the President on domestic policy and be responsible for White House operations in all substantive matters concerning domestic affairs." Daniel P. Moynihan, previously the assistant for urban affairs and executive secretary of the Cabinet-level Urban Affairs Council, and Bryce N. Harlow, the assistant for congressional relations, become "Counsellors to the President, with Cabinet rank." Their primary function will be "to anticipate events, to think through the consequences of current trends, to question conventional wisdom, to address fundamentals and to stimulate long-range innovation." Six other assistants, variously titled and already on the staff, are to form and head, under Ehrlichman's direction, temporary "project groups" which will "conduct research and present policy options to the President." Every policy recommendation that requires the President's approval or disapproval, whether it originates within the White House system, anywhere in the vast complex of domestic departments and agencies, or from numerous unofficial study groups that are always at work on policy problems, is to reach Mr. Nixon only after it has been thoroughly staffed out by the Ehrlichman team and cleared by Ehrlichman himself. The two new Counsellors, Cabinet officers and the heads of major independent agencies may submit ideas, orally or in writing, directly to the President, but only if they do not call for his formal approval or disapproval in a way affecting basic policy. After material policy matters, domestic or foreign, have been through the Ehrlichman and Kissinger mills, they must still—as in the past—survive the scrutiny of H. R. (Bob) Haldeman, the President's managerial chief of staff, and his small secretariat.

The new element in Mr. Nixon's "struggle for neatness" is the sweeping power of review and initial selection now granted to the Assistant for Domestic Affairs. Who, then, is John Ehrlichman? Perhaps more to the point, who was he before he turned

up at the Nixon White House? The available answers are interesting because they come to so very little. He is a Christian
Scientist, aged 44, a stocky and personable and manifestly intelligent lawyer from Seattle. He specialized there in zoning and
land-use law. He is said to have been extremely competent and
successful at it. A Republican, he took no discernible interest
and no part in the politics of Seattle and Washington State although his uncle, Ben Ehrlichman, is a rich and active Republican
who ranks with the state party's five or six biggest money-raisers.
Youngish Republicans of John Ehrlichman's generation worked
mightily to get Dan Evans, one of their kind, elected governor
of the state in 1964. As Evans and the others frequently reflect
nowadays, John Ehrlichman stood aside. Evans barely knows
him, even now, and one of the state's highest Republican officials
met Ehrlichman for the first time at the White House just the
other day. Reporters searching for something positive to say of
his earlier phase have noted that as a lawyer he represented con-
servationist groups against land despoilers. Ehrlichman has the
grace to be slightly embarrassed, explaining that he did this in
only two cases of any importance and, far more often, represented
clients on the other side. His experience with urban zoning taught
him that real estate practices have a good deal to do with the
plight of slum dwellers and aroused a certain sympathy for the
urban poor, but he disclaims any strong ideological bent along
this or any other line.

Why was he the political neuter that he cheerfully admits he
was in his home city and state? Ehrlichman answered my question
for quotation, something he rarely does. What the first part of
his answer came down to was that his interest is not in politics
as such, Republican or otherwise, but in Richard Nixon. At the
urging of Bob Haldeman, whom he had known at college in
California, Ehrlichman took leave from his law practice for six
months to work for Nixon in the Presidential campaign of 1960.
He has helped, mostly as a tour organizer, in every Nixon campaign since, including Nixon's interim campaigning for Republican state and congressional candidates. In that work, Ehrlichman
says, "I had all the political satisfaction I needed, and I had all
the political activity my practice could stand." The second part
of his answer was: "I had the kind of law practice where I had

to avoid political animosities because I was dealing with county officials in most of the courthouses in the state of Washington, particularly in western Washington, and they were mostly Democrats, and I was also dealing with Senators and Congressmen."

Nixon's yen for neatness was apparent before he took office. Kissinger's success in creating the appearance of it in the foreign policy process strengthened the President's conviction that it ought to be attainable, somehow, on the domestic side, and his growing impression that Ehrlichman was the man to achieve it for him has been evident for months. An authoritative account of the President's feelings on the subject tells more about Mr. Nixon than the changes and new appointments do in themselves, and it runs as follows.

Early on, it is said at the White House, Nixon got and resented a feeling that sizable staffs working under various assistants were busy with duplicating and overlapping ideas, proposals, programs. A variety of options, and strong advocacy of those options, were good things in themselves, but it increasingly seemed to the President that there was an excess of both. He came to feel that a lot of time in the echelons below him, and a lot of his own time, was needlessly lost in resolving that excess of conflicting viewpoints. The several Cabinet sub-groups that he had instituted and announced with pride—the Urban Affairs Council, a Cabinet Committee on Economic Policy, an Environmental Council—seemed to him to be compounding disorder rather than producing the ordered flow he had anticipated. A tentative and limited grant of authority to Ehrlichman in early March to coordinate the incoming mass of program paper helped some, but not enough. A small Domestic Affairs Council, set up without fanfare at the turn of May–June, became the vehicle for trial-and-error stabs at the fuller coordination and concentration of program preparation that Nixon sought.

On a Saturday afternoon toward the end of his California interlude in August and September, the President spent three and one-half hours chewing at the problem with Ehrlichman and urging him to get something definitive and workable done about it. Nixon said during this conversation that he had spent many hours discussing techniques of policy formulation with Henry Kissinger and simply couldn't believe that a domestic process at least roughly

equivalent to Kissinger's could not be devised. Ehrlichman, Haldeman, Bryce Harlow, and others produced some recommendations
soon after the return from California. They coincided in some
respects with the suggestions of an executive commission study-
ing governmental organization as a whole. Nixon said in effect
in late October—*enough,* let's do *something*—and out came this
elaborate reach for a neatness that Mr. Nixon wants, will continue to want and, predictably, will never get.

XVI

Without Warts

It's fun, watching Dick capture Teddy, if you ignore the stretches of awful writing in *The Making of the President 1968* ("... there was a drama in the man, in his turning-about in himself; but it was a drama too dense for easy analysis") and follow Theodore H. White's account of the process by which he was brought to discover in himself "a slow and ever-growing respect" for Richard Nixon. As *the* chronicler of Presidential campaigns since 1960, White saw more of Nixon in person during and after the 1968 campaign than any other journalist did and the resultant sketches are, for me, the parts of this third *Making of the President* that repay the effort it takes to work through the whole. There are many fine descriptive passages, including a superlative account of Robert Kennedy's aborted campaign, but they are so buried amongst and clouded by the author's attempts to make lasting history of his reportage that reading his book becomes a chore. Those who skip it will miss a great deal that is interesting and evocative of a turning year in American politics. But they will miss very little that would add to their understanding of that year, and they will spare themselves passages that add only to a misunderstanding of it and of the President it produced.

Teddy's natural preference, his hero in 1960, was John F. Kennedy, as Robert Kennedy was in 1968. Nixon, observed from a distance in 1960, seemed to White to be banal, self-pitying, petulant but never (he says now) untrustworthy, cowardly, or stupid. Beginning in November of 1967, Nixon saw to it that White observed him at close and occasionally intimate vantage. A first meeting in Nixon's New York apartment was cordial enough but "wary, brisk and businesslike." Next came—by chance, White says—a sharing of seats on a commercial shuttle flight from Washington to New York and a ride together from the airport into the city. They talked about writing ("how, when, at what times of day did I work—where?"); at Teddy's instance, about Isaac Newton ("he wanted to hear more about Newton, all about Newton"); at Nixon's instance, about "the marvel" of training raw girls to be skilled airline hostesses; about Presidential politics and polls, Nixon impressing Teddy with "clear, detached, lucid summaries of the problems of all the candidates." Nixon left White on that day with "a new view of the Nixon personality— in which the trait uppermost was a voracious, almost insatiable curiosity of mind, a hunger to know, to learn, to find out how things work, to understand and explore detail." They met again on the following March 12, the day of Nixon's and Eugene McCarthy's victories in the New Hampshire primaries. Nixon was "in his nervous mood," preoccupied with Vietnam (how could the next President, how would Teddy "liquidate that war with honor"?) and with the indications, soon realized, that Nelson Rockefeller would try for the Republican nomination. Nixon had previously asked Teddy whether he thought Rockefeller "would make a good Secretary of State." Now their talk went "back and forth, between the probable results and impact of the New Hampshire primary on the Republican Party and the great external world." It was warming, it was effective. At this stage of their acquaintance, Teddy writes, "I came to believe that one must respect this man: there was about all he said a conviction and a sincerity . . . There was in all he said, even in discussing the most hostile personalities, a total absence of bitterness, of the rancor and venom that had once colored his remarks."

The acquaintance throve—aboard Nixon's campaign plane and at Nixon's post-election headquarters in New York, with an inter-

view that produced one of the book's better passages. The country
needed, the President-elect wanted to give it "a sense of purpose,
a sense of a binding ideal. . . . Did I remember the kick-off of
the campaign? The phrase he had used in the opening speech at
(*sic*) New Hampshire—'the country needs the lift of a driving
dream'? That's what he was looking for." At the last meeting
reported in the book, in the Oval Office at the White House on
the Thursday after the Inauguration, President Nixon "was calm
as I had never seen him before, as if peace had settled on him."
He showed his guest the agenda of his first Cabinet meeting,
talked of how he proposed to use *his* Cabinet and *his* National
Security Council, and displayed to Teddy "an executive mind at
work, with logic, force, and clarity."

It is well that we have, from a journalist not previously entranced with Richard Nixon, so friendly and confident a portrait
of the President, and this reader is grateful to Teddy White for
it. I wish that as much could be said for the book in the whole.
One sentence in it, on page 363 of the first edition, encapsulates
the several vices of style and judgment that, for me, disqualify the
book as "A narrative history of American politics in action"—
the subtitle on the jacket—and suggest that Teddy White paid
a large price for his access to Nixon and to the Oval Office. The
sentence is as follows: "In 1968, Nixon conspicuously, con-
scientiously, calculatedly denied himself all racist votes, yielding
them to Wallace." That is not true. It would not be true if the
three adverbs (in a sentence of 15 words!) were omitted. The
opposite is true: the President is paying now, in other coin, for
the appeal that he in fact made for Wallace votes. White's entire
account of this aspect of the Nixon campaign is in keeping with
the quoted sentence. It is as if Teddy throughout the campaign
were deaf to the code in which Nixon spoke on this matter and
blind to those qualities in Richard Nixon which made it possible
for him to speak in that code.

XVII

Nixon Through the Tube

The Selling of the President 1968 is the best thing that's happened to Richard Nixon since somebody told him to stop wiggling those fingers. The author, Joe McGinniss, has done the President the immense and obviously unintended favor of showing him to be the normal, temperish, profane, vulnerable adult male that his spokesmen at the White House keep insisting he isn't. They are under the illusion that Mr. Nixon is best served by making him out to be superhumanly calm, beyond disturbance—a Presidential potato. On September 23, for instance, Press Secretary Ronald Ziegler denied a report that the President had been "infuriated" by premature disclosure of his plans for troop withdrawal from Vietnam, and brought on the following exchange with correspondents:

Q.: Nothing has angered or upset him?
Ziegler: I haven't seen him angered or upset at all.

Q.: For how long a time?

Ziegler: For quite a while—since January 20.

Joe McGinniss informs us—and accurately, I am told by some of the men who figure in this book and who still work for Nixon —that he wasn't like that during the 1968 campaign. At a TV taping session in October, he referred to "the damn Negro-Puerto Rican groups" who were trying to get control of their public schools in New York City and said to Frank Shakespeare, a CBS executive who now is Nixon's United States Information Agency director: "I don't care whether they're white or whoever the hell they are. When they hit the teachers over the head, goddamit, they have no right to run the school." He remarked on another occasion that a hostile questioner on one of his staged TV panel shows could have "screwed" him. Frank Shakespeare thought Nixon capable of saying—"in private, of course," under sufficient provocation from the printed press—that "those liberal bastards are fucking me again."

Shakespeare and the other campaign staffers who managed the Nixon TV effort last year would have saved themselves a lot of pain and deprived us of the most interesting account yet written of the 1968 race for the Presidency if they had troubled to check on the beguiling young man (aged 26) who presented himself to them in June. As they recall it, he said that he wanted to research and write a studious, philosophic account of the role of the electronic media in modern Presidential politics. No quotes; nothing that would embarrass anybody; a book, they were led to expect, that would deal in soporific generalities and take them and their expertise with stultifying gravity. Any Philadelphia journalist, or indeed any reader of McGinniss' column in the *Philadelphia Inquirer,* could have told them how ludicrous this was. McGinniss was known in Philadelphia as something of a journalistic prodigy, a sharpshooter with minimal regard for reportorial niceties and a special appeal to young readers. His disrespectful treatment of the city police had alienated his publisher, Walter Annenberg (now Nixon's Ambassador to Great Britain), leading to rumors that Annenberg was about to leave McGinniss when McGinniss left Annenberg in order to write the book. The fact seems to be that Joe McGinniss did a thorough job of conning Shakespeare;

Leonard Garment, a Nixon law partner who supervised the pro-
motional experts and is now one of the more intelligent White
House assistants; Harry Treleaven, a hotshot advertising man who
for a time directed the Republican National Committee's public
relations; and, from a distance, the awesome John Mitchell, now
the Attorney General and, according to the President, his closest
domestic adviser. Garment, Treleaven, and Shakespeare admitted
McGinniss to their private councils, let him observe the electronic
promotion of Candidate Nixon at first hand, and lately have had
the pleasure of reading some of their confidential memos to each
other in the book's appendix.

I am supposed, I gather, to be frightened by the evidence in
those documents and in McGinniss' rich store of intimate quota-
tions that enormous thought and effort went into remaking Richard
Nixon for television and into projecting an image so different from
"the real Nixon" as to constitute a massive fraud upon the electorate. In that exercise, McGinniss suggests, we have the ultimate
fulfillment of the worst conceptions of Marshall McLuhan and
of Daniel Boorstin, whose testaments to the shaping power of
television are frequently cited. Well, after reading and rereading
the McGinniss account, I am reassured. It didn't work. All of
that effort, all of those millions spent for television accomplished
—what? Essentially the same Richard Nixon whom I followed
in person around the country came across to the country through

the tube. Frank Shakespeare is quoted as saying early in the
campaign that "without television he wouldn't have a chance.
With it, he cannot lose." With it, he very nearly lost and for this,
according to McGinniss, there was a reason that in my opinion
does Nixon credit. After a period of initial uncertainty, when he
was telling the TV boys, "You fellows just tell me what you want
me to do and I'll do it," he rebelled and insisted on being himself again. McGinniss, reflecting the outrage of his television pals,
tells what began to happen in September:

> So Nixon began to pull back. The desperation he had felt in early
> spring was gone. He was leading now. He was going to win. He would
> continue to run a television campaign, yes; it was the easiest way to
> dodge the press. But he would do it his way from now on. . . . He
> would show them he could be just as dull and artificial on television
> as he had ever been in person.

He'd never been anything else, in fact, and he still is that in the
Presidency, at the White House on observed occasions, and at
his press conferences and other televised appearances. It is for the
unobserved but overheard and intimately quoted Nixon that I
value the McGinniss account. It is useful to know that the President has a horror of psychiatrists—Leonard Garment vetoed the
appearance of one on a Nixon campaign show—and that he
curses when he's angry. Whatever we have in the Nixon Presidency, we don't have a potato. Maybe Nixon should hire Joe
McGinniss.

XVIII

Students

At the White House on Saturday afternoon, September 20, President Nixon spent an hour and 40 minutes with some 225 college and university students. He talked to them, he talked with them, and he let them talk to him. It was a unique occasion, the first of its kind since he was nominated for the Presidency, and the President was at one with most of his guests in judging afterward that it was a considerable success.

It should have been. Months of inquiry and preparation preceded it, and more months of evasion of anything approaching confrontation with the student generation came before that. Reporters who covered Mr. Nixon's 1968 campaign can never forget his demeaning flight from a crowd of polite and passive students massed on the campus of William and Mary College at Williamsburg, Va., after addressing a small group of them at a closed meeting. A taped interview with four sedate youngsters brought to Williamsburg from other colleges was never televised. A couple of groups of student opponents of the Vietnam war met at the White House with Henry A. Kissinger, the President's staff adviser on foreign policy. Charles B. (Bud) Wilkinson, the former

Oklahoma football coach who is Mr. Nixon's special consultant for youth affairs, and his staff of recent graduates have been meeting, mostly in secret, with student groups around the country and presumably conveying their wants and plaints to the President. But his own student contacts since his Inauguration have been confined, so far as is known, to the speeches he delivered in June, on his way to Midway Island, at General Beadle State College in South Dakota and at the Air Force Academy in Colorado Springs. Neither encounter dispelled the impression that Mr. Nixon was afraid of students and of the disruptive effects that they, in uncontrolled situations and numbers, might have upon him and upon his efforts to lower the national fevers.

This is not an impression that the President and his assistants want to encourage, and Bud Wilkinson and some others on the White House staff had been on the alert for a chance to correct it. They detected the possible makings of that chance when they heard about the plans of the Association of Student Governments for a national conference at which the presidents of student bodies and the presidents of colleges and universities would get together for a discussion of campus problems. The ASG is, by definition, an organization of students who have made it on their campuses. Its members are the elected presidents of their student "governments." Along with their campus organizations they are, more often than not, as much on the defensive against campus revolutionaries as their college and university administrations are. The national headquarters is in Washington, in an office building three blocks from the White House. Edward (Ned) Callan, a senior on leave from Colorado State College and ASG's acting president, struck a responsive chord at the White House with a speech, later to become the printed theme of the conference, entitled "Evolution Not Revolution: A Time for Constructive Activism." He and his associates on the ASG national staff welcomed initial inquiries from Wilkinson and from Tom Huston, a young Nixon speech writer, about the possibilities of somehow tying the White House into the proposed "Presidents to Presidents" conference. Its declared purpose—"To Seek the Answers Together"—was pleasantly in tune with the "Bring Us Together" theme proclaimed by Mr. Nixon on the day after his election.

Months of rather wary negotiation followed, through the summer and early fall, while the ASG staff digested the replies from some 1,300 invited institutions and the final acceptances from about 225 of them. A condition was that the student presidents had to be accompanied to the conference in Washington by either the president or a responsible administrator of their schools, and most of the institutions that met the requirement turned out to be among the country's smaller colleges and universities. The program was weighted (or so the ASG staff thought) against set speeches and toward discussion sessions with panels of government officials, educators, business and labor spokesmen. With one exception, invited speakers were told they would be expected to answer questions from their audience.

The exception was Mr. Nixon. The matter of audience questioning was not raised when he was invited during the summer. He neither rejected nor accepted the invitation when, in a "Dear Herman" letter in August from his Western White House to Herman Pirchner, Jr., ASG's executive secretary, he applauded the idea of the conference, endorsed the thought that "the university must be in the vanguard of reform," and noted a belief that "the overwhelming majority of today's youth are responsible, sincere, and concerned citizens." Whether he would agree to meet ASG's responsible, sincere, and concerned citizens was still uncertain at the start of the conference week. Too late for notation in the printed program, John Campbell (Duke '66) and Jeffrey Donfeld (UCLA '65, Berkeley Law '68) of the Wilkinson staff intimated on Tuesday of that week that the President would prefer to meet the students and their accompanying administrators in the White House East Room. The ASG staff thought it was settled then, and passed the word to the assembling conferees, but the White House staff did not consider the engagement binding until the afternoon before the event.

The meeting could have gone badly wrong. Forty or so of the student delegates, hotted up by a few black students from "black" colleges and warmly supported by white rebels of like mind, had been protesting since the conference opened that they had not come to Washington to be talked at by official and other dignitaries, but to talk at them and among each other. They wanted to talk about American society and what it was doing to American campuses, not about the campuses as isolated problem centers.

Some of them had proposed to boycott the White House meeting and, dissuaded from that, had given the ASG staff and one of their morning guests, federal Education Commissioner James E. Allen, Jr., a rough time. They had demanded and had been denied hard answers, then and there, to hard questions—such as whether, and when, and with what amounts of money the federal government was going to do something about the growing difficulties of small colleges, black and white. Vietnam, the draft, drugs-on-campus, "institutional racism" were also on their minds, boiling up at the conference, and among the President's guests there were dissidents who complained, with mounting anger, that their questions had been neither discussed nor answered satisfactorily. Later that afternoon at the conference and through the night that followed, they raised vocal hell.

But not in the East Room, not at the White House and not with the President. Mr. Nixon and his staff had figured correctly in calculating the effect of this place upon this group. His graceful little speech with its softening message—the way to be effective is to be *quiet*—went over well and drew sustained applause at the end. Beside his daughter Tricia, all in pink and blonde and lovely and attentive, he afterward shook hands and had a brief word with everybody there (excepting a few who refused to join the line). Presidential assistants, among them no less a personage than Counsellor Arthur Burns, the distinguished economist, sought out the student guests, individually and in clusters, and gave respectful heed to whatever they had to say. Lou Oates from Central State College in Ohio, one of the black dissidents, paused before the President and talked at him for a minute or so, emphasizing what he said with a thrusting arm—but, as the onlookers could see, with courtesy too. The President halted Marvin L. Peebles (Penn State '66, Villanova Law '69), the ASG staff's black specialist in student rights, for a few extra seconds of talk. Did Mr. Nixon, toward the end of an hour and 25 minutes of such encounters, take in what was said to him? Peebles said afterward that he didn't know, couldn't tell, but he did know that he and most of the others were pleased.

It happened that, a couple of days later, the President announced and Counsellor Burns explained the formation of a new batch of task forces to develop long range policies for Mr. Nixon. One of them would deal with "priorities in higher education" and the provision of larger opportunities "for students from minority and low income backgrounds." Burns was asked whether students would be represented on this task force. "As presently planned," he answered, "it will consist principally of university and college presidents."

XIX

Haynsworth

From 11:18 to 11:45 on the morning of October 20, President Nixon showed himself, in person, to White House reporters in his Oval Office. There were no cameras, no microphones, no tape recorders, not even the Signal Corps recorder that is usually at work in case the stenotypist misses something said at special White House briefings for the press. There were just Mr. Nixon, his press secretary standing off to one side, White House Counsel John Ehrlichman slouched in silence on a sofa at the rear, and some 40 reporters standing in front of the President's desk, facing him. This had happened only once before, on the morning after the President nominated Warren Burger to be Chief Justice of the United States, and that had been a very different occasion. It had been preceded, the evening before, by a great nomination show on national television, and the President had called in reporters to discuss his choice, and brag about it a little, confident that no serious objections would be raised to it. He said now that he had called us in to discuss "the Haynsworth matter," a Supreme Court nomination to which serious and possibly decisive objections had been raised.

It occurred to me, watching Mr. Nixon and hearing him out, that the critical differences between this nomination and the previous one must have been apparent to the President since August. He was vacationing in California then. His nominee, Judge Clement F. Haynsworth Jr., had remained at his home in South Carolina and the President had remained secluded in his office at San Clemente when the nomination was announced with a written handout. They talked by telephone that day, and that was all—because, it was suggested then, Judge Haynsworth stammered slightly and would be uncomfortable at a joint appearance. They were said to have never met, certainly not during Nixon's Presidency, and the President, disclaiming any "political obligation to select Judge Haynsworth," was able to say on October 20 that "if he would walk into this room, I am afraid I wouldn't recognize him." This he said, in a manner and a tone indicating that he thought he was making a crucial point about a judge of whom he also said:

> I have read the income tax returns, the financial statements, all the charges . . . I find that Judge Haynsworth is an honest man. I find that he has been, in my opinion as a lawyer, a lawyer's lawyer and a judge's judge. I think he will be a great credit to the Supreme Court, and I am going to stand by him until he is confirmed. I trust he will be.

The President was standing behind his desk. His hands—you learn to watch the Nixon hands—at this moment were clasped over the top edges of his black reclining chair, not tightly as they so often are clasped, but loosely. Never once during the 27 minutes was he seen, as he often is, to halt his hands in mid-course from back to front, from belt to chin level, tips touching, and hold them rigid while he *thinks*—what to do with them next? Here, we were entitled to suppose, was the Nixon who impresses his friends, his staff, his Cabinet associates with his sincerity, his competence, his command of himself. Here, too, was Nixon under stress, putting himself and his judgment, his standards of honor and judicial ethics on the line for a Supreme Court nominee who was in bad trouble along with, as Nixon now said, "the President of the United States who nominated him in the first place."

A few things, little things, marred the performance. One of them, we were asked to believe later, was not the President's

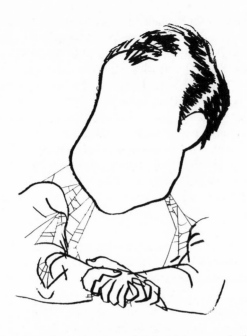

doing. The transcript, the record for history and the one that appeared in newspaper texts, was imperfect because (we were told) the stenotypist didn't hear all that was said. The President, referring to Judge Haynsworth's embarrassing and extensive stock portfolio and a suggestion that he and other judges put their holdings in trust, said he thought it was better to "own nothing but real estate," as Mr. Nixon did, unless—wryly—the real estate happened to be near a government installation. This reference to his new California estate, conveniently adjoining a Coast Guard station, is not in the transcript. Nixon said that even if Judge Haynsworth asked that his nomination be withdrawn, "I would not let him do it." The permanent record has it that the President himself "would not do so." A reporter asked Nixon what he replied to people who said that he had "selected Haynsworth in large part because of political obligations to Southerners and conservatives." The record omits "to Southerners and conservatives." Nixon replied as if he hadn't heard that part, either, reducing the question to whether he had or hadn't known Haynsworth.

The President overreached in other ways, so minor that they went largely unnoticed in the news accounts. He referred twice to "Judge Marlow Cook," meaning the freshman Republican senator from Kentucky who is leading the Senate defense of Haynsworth. "He was a judge before he became a senator, as you know," Nixon remarked by way of adding to Cook's authority in the matter. Marlow Cook was a county judge, in Kentucky an administrative and not a judicial office. Nixon picked out and made absurdly much of two petty items from Senator Cook's massive refutation of charges that Haynsworth had let his investments affect his judicial decisions. One of the items concerned the 1000 shares of Brunswick Corporation stock that Haynsworth bought while a trivial case involving that company was before his court. Nixon solemnly quoted Cook to the effect that if the entire benefit from the favorable decision had accrued to Brunswick stockholders—which, as Cook had said, could not have happened—"Judge Haynsworth would have profited by $5 at the most, probably $4.92, the exact figure." Using the same standard in another case, Nixon said that "Judge Haynsworth's stock would have been reduced in value by 48 cents as a result of the decision that he made." The serious question was whether a judge who is fitted for the Supreme Court would have bought the Brunswick stock when Haynsworth did. Nixon skipped it.

The President showed himself in better though hardly unassailable form when he dealt with two other issues raised by the Haynsworth affair. They went, as he put it, "to what senators should consider as they determine whether to confirm a judge for the Supreme Court, or, for that matter, any court." A nominee's judicial philosophy, he said, is not "a proper ground" for acceptance or rejection by senators. He recalled that Louis Brandeis ("among my heroes of the Court") was almost voted down by senators who thought him "too liberal." Charles Evans Hughes was all but denied confirmation "because he was too conservative" and because, "like Judge Haynsworth," he had represented various business interests. In part and properly, however, Nixon had selected Judge Haynsworth for the Supreme Court because he "had a philosophy for the Constitution similar to my own because that is what a President is expected to do." He elaborated in terms that would be remembered in connection with him and his Presidency, regardless of how the Haynsworth matter came out: ". . . If Judge Haynsworth's philosophy leans to the conservative side, in my view that recommends him to me. . . It is the Judge's responsibility, and the Supreme Court's responsibility, to interpret the Constitution and interpret the law, and not to go beyond that in putting his own socioeconomic philosophy into decisions in a way that goes beyond the law, beyond the Constitution." He had begun to "balance" the present court against that tendency with the Burger nomination, and he said now that he proposed to balance it further with the Haynsworth nomination. No Senator, the President was saying, should oppose the nomination because he didn't think the Court should be "balanced" that way.

The other issue was whether "the appearance of impropriety . . . is enough to disqualify a man." Mr. Nixon may be read in his total remarks to have argued that "the appearance of impropriety" in Judge Haynsworth's case had been demolished. But he didn't say that at this point and in so many words. He said that this standard "would mean that anybody who wants to make a charge can thereby create the appearance of impropriety, raise a doubt, and that then his [a nominee's] name should be withdrawn." It was one of the elisions, one of the flaws, in a generally impressive and fascinating performance that left me wondering whether Mr. Nixon was as certain about Clement Haynsworth as he tried to appear to be.

———

On November 21, the Senate refused, 55 to 45, to confirm the nomination.

XX

The Veep

One of the nicer people at the Nixon White House is Mrs. Alice Fringer, Vice President Spiro T. Agnew's secretary. She has known him since he joined her late husband's Baltimore law firm 25 years ago, she has been his secretary since he began his public career seven years ago as the managing executive of Baltimore County, and she does not take any guff from him. On a February day, in the White House office where Vice President Agnew was quartered at President Nixon's order, Mrs. Fringer asked Agnew how he liked the job. "Very much," he answered. She said that he could tell her the truth: did he *really* like it? "I'm telling you the truth," he replied, "I really do."

Mrs. Fringer and the 12 other principal members of the Vice President's personal staff liked it better than they did in the first two months when he was freed from the elegant thralldom imposed upon him by the original White House arrangement. They rejected the notion, popular with the press, that Nixon put Agnew in the West Wing of the White House, only three offices removed from the President's own Oval Room, more to keep him on a tight tether than to dignify the Vice Presidency. Their objection,

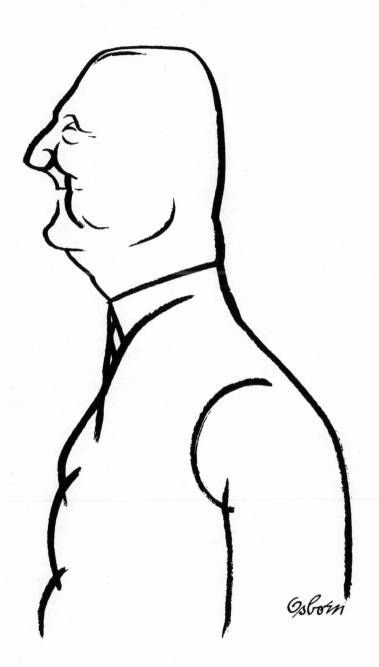

grounded in observable fact, was that being there was a nuisance
to him and to his assistants, all of whom excepting Mrs. Fringer
were quartered in the neighboring Executive Office Building. After
Agnew moved in March into an ample office there, complete with
such amenities as a kitchenette and dressing room, he and his
assistants had a much easier time of it. He retained the West
Wing office, for the reception of honored callers and for the very
rare occasions when the President wished to be near his Vice
President. They continued to meet regularly at Cabinet, NSC,
Urban Affairs Council, and similar sessions, and the Vice President spoke with touching pleasure of a few evening engagements,
formal and informal, at the Presidential mansion. But the President's necessary rationing of his time did not provide much of
it for intimate converse with the Vice President.

This could be misinterpreted. Nixon was a Vice President for
eight years, he has studied the history of his office with the greatest care, and he may be assumed to have absorbed the lesson
that Harry Truman set forth in his memoirs after he left the
Presidency. The lesson is that Presidents and Vice Presidents are
happy together only when they are not too much together. Old
hands at the White House have watched Eisenhower, then John
Kennedy, and then Lyndon Johnson, undertake to share their
Presidencies to the fullest with their Vice Presidents and discover,
the hard way for both parties, that Presidents simply do not have
the time and energy to spare for frequent personal involvement
with a subordinate who is, however strenuous the effort to inflate
his job, fundamentally superfluous until that moment when he
may suddenly be essential. The end result, particularly painful in
the recent cases of Vice Presidents Johnson and Hubert Humphrey, has been frustration, hidden bitterness, and public embarrassment for both men. Under Nixon, the outward inflation
continued with announcements that Agnew was to preside at
Cabinet, NSC, Cabinet committee, and Urban Council meetings
when the President was absent and to head a new Office of Inter-
Governmental Relations, concerned with the federal interests of
state, city, and county governments. But President Nixon, who
prefers written communication with his own assistants and avoids
personal contact with them whenever possible, neither undertook
publicly nor acted privately to buddy up with his Vice President.

At meetings in the Cabinet Room, Nixon and Agnew sit opposite each other at the center of the Cabinet table, with the ranking department Secretaries present to the right and left of the President. When Agnew entered the Cabinet Room to preside over an early session of the Council on Urban Affairs in Nixon's absence, someone suggested that he take the President's chair. "Oh, no," he said, "that's for the President," and he proceeded to conduct the meeting from his usual place. He did it with ease and competence, according to Nixon assistants who were present. As a participant, under the President's eye, he is said to give every evidence of confidence and of familiarity with the business at hand. "He certainly does his share of talking," a White House assistant who has observed him at meetings says. "I get the impression," says another, "that he is quite a quick study."

A Vice President's sole constitutional duty is to preside over the Senate. Agnew, the first Vice President since 1945 who has not been a Senator, probably would be reasonably content if this were his only mandatory duty. He tried initially to reserve at least three hours of his crowded days for opening each Senate session, building up friendships with Senators of both parties, and mastering the Senate's rules and customs. His first Capitol Hill mentors were Senator Everett M. Dirksen, the Minority Leader, and Walter Mote, who represented the Republican minority on the Senate Rules Committee staff for eleven years and was recommended to Agnew by Bryce Harlow, the President's assistant for Congressional affairs, who had intended to hire Mote for his own staff. His legislative assistant, stationed with Mote on Capitol Hill, was Frank De Costa, a young Negro attorney from Baltimore, who was Agnew's civil-rights adviser in the two years when he was governor of Maryland. De Costa disclaimed any special concern with minority matters in Washington and referred inquiries on that subject to Herbert Thompson, Agnew's press assistant.

De Costa and Thompson were among the nine assistants, including Mrs. Fringer, who worked for Agnew when he was governor and accompanied him to Washington. Their chief and Agnew's senior assistant was C. Stanley Blair, who was Maryland's Secretary of State and, in effect, a lieutenant governor without the right of succession during Agnew's abbreviated term. Only three of Agnew's assistants knew much more about Washington than he did as of January 20. They were Walter Mote; Kent Crane, a young Foreign Service man on loan from the State Department; and C. D. Ward, a Washington attorney who had been general counsel for the National Association of Counties and had a lot to do with establishing the Office of Inter-Governmental Relations. The newcomers, like their boss, gave an impression of earnest effort to learn.

Agnew appeared during the first months to be increasingly at ease with himself, his President, and his difficult job, in a guarded sort of way. He and Nixon had an understanding that the Vice President in his speeches and at his few press conferences would confine himself either to orthodox generalities or to the particulars of his assigned concerns. He displayed a rather appealing awareness of the handicaps that he brought upon himself with his awkward performance during the 1968 campaign and especially of his low standing—even lower than the President's—with black Americans. In the only interview he granted during his first four weeks in office, he told Jack Germond of the Gannett Newspapers that "I don't see any use of my protesting any more that it's all wrong, that they had me pegged wrong. I couldn't possibly convince them of that by just saying it." He expected, he said, to spend more time on federal efforts to improve the lot of the black poor than on anything else and his close attention to the work and problems of the Urban Council suggested that this was so.

Watching Vice President Agnew in his early appearances in President Nixon's company made for an odd impression. A stranger to the United States and to them could have supposed that Agnew with his straight stance, his pomaded greying hair, his look of restrained dignity and self-possession was the President being nice to the man who, at any moment and for better or worse, might be the next President.

XXI

Agnew's Mission

Mr. Nixon's chief assistants heard an interesting report from Omaha on October 27. The occasion was their daily staff meeting, the reporter was James Keogh, and his subject was Vice President Spiro T. Agnew. Keogh, a former Omaha newspaperman and *Time* editor who heads up the stable of Nixon writers, had been back to Omaha for a dinner in his honor and he had been exposed to a lot of talk from a lot of people about the Vice President. "It astonished me, the strength of the pro-Agnew thing," Keogh said in summarizing what he had told his White House associates. "I sensed the feeling of people who felt that the Vice President was saying what they would like to say." One of the remarks that Keogh quoted, a reference to Agnew's ancestry, made the White House rounds and may be supposed to have reached the President. It was that "Spiro Agnew is the noblest Greek of them all."

Harry Dent, Senator Strom Thurmond's gift to the White House staff and the President's political coordinator, brought similar tidings from California. At a state Republican dinner in Sacramento, and at party meetings elsewhere, the loudest and longest applause was for any mention of the Vice President. Dent concluded, and reported when he returned, that Agnew was saying the kind of things Republicans wanted to hear and felt that they hadn't been hearing often and clearly enough to suit them from the Nixon Administration. Dent's special task during the 1968 campaign had been to lure Southern Democrats away from George C. Wallace and deliver them to Nixon, and he judged during his California trip that Agnew was well on his way toward performing a similar service on a national scale in 1970 and 1972.

Letters and telegrams addressed to Agnew from around the country supported this conclusion. They had been coming in at the modest rate of 1500 per week. The week's count on October 31 showed 4395 applauding and 1251 criticizing his recent line of talk. Most of them were in response to a speech that he had delivered in New Orleans on Sunday night, October 19, and the sentence that elicited most of the response was as follows: "A spirit of national masochism prevails, encouraged by an effete corps of impudent snobs who characterize themselves as intellectuals." He also said:

> We seem to be approaching an age of the gross. Persuasion . . . is too often discarded for disruptive demonstrations. . . . Those who claim to speak for the young . . . overwhelm themselves with drugs and artificial stimulants. . . . Life is visceral rather than intellectual, and the most visceral practitioners of life are those who characterize themselves as intellectuals. . . . Education is being redefined . . . to suit the ideas of the uneducated. . . . The lessons of the past are ignored and obliterated in a contemporary antagonism known as the generation gap.

Then he made his central point: "The recent Vietnam Moratorium is a reflection of the confusion that exists in America today." It was outrageous, he implied, that "thousands of well-motivated young people" had been led to participate in "a massive public outpouring of sentiment against the foreign policy of the President of the United States," and worse that those who so misled the young had "refused to disassociate themselves from the objectives enunciated by the enemy in Hanoi." Still worse was to come in mid-November, promoted by "the hardcore dissidents and the professional anarchists within the so-called 'peace movement'—wilder, more violent, and equally barren of constructive result."

The reference to "impudent snobs" dominated the Monday morning news accounts, and the first reaction at the White House was informative. The President's writers, who have occasionally reviewed and touched up Agnew speeches, put it about that they had had nothing to do with this one. Other Nixon assistants encountered that day were heard to moan that Spiro had said the right thing in the wrong way. The usual curtain hid Nixon's reaction: it was said for him only that the Vice President was and

always had been "free to speak for himself." The Nixon people were not at all sorry that the furor over the New Orleans speech diverted attention from one that Agnew made in Jackson, Miss., on the Monday night. There he told 2400 Mississippians who had paid $100 a plate to hear him that, "for too long the South has been punching the bag for those who characterize themselves as liberal intellectuals." He said that "these leaders on the New Left" are "taking control of the national Democratic party" and associated them with "the group that believes in marching down the streets of America to protest the war in Vietnam to our President."

It was a full week and more before the tone of White House comment changed. When it did, the change was something to sense and observe. Keogh's report from Nebraska, Dent's from California, and the gradual rise in the flow of applauding letters and telegrams convinced the Nixon people that Agnew was suddenly an asset instead of the liability that many of them had thought him to be. The note of condescension that hitherto had marked the most respectful references to him vanished. Instead of apologies for his naivete, his insensitivity to the nuances of national and Washington politics, there was word from quarters as close as you can get to the President without entering his Oval Office that the Vice President "had the green light." It was said on equally good authority that Agnew was speaking for and to "Middle America" —to those "forgotten Americans" who had previously been wooed and supposedly won by Nixon himself and who, it was now suspected, had been disappointed in their hopes that the President would speak to them as Agnew was talking to them for him.

Was Agnew in fact speaking for Nixon, upon the President's authority? Of course he was, but the question persisted and was allowed to play a part in heightening press and national awareness of and interest in the Vice President. On the night of his return from New Orleans and Jackson, Agnew met and talked with the President at a White House dinner and said afterward that his speeches and the response to them were not mentioned. The same word went out after a meeting the next week with the President and the Republican Congressional leadership. It was not until the morning of October 30, at a Republican party reception in the White House Mansion, that Nixon tired of the game and went out of his way to say that his Vice President was "doing a great job for the Administration." Agnew by then had composed the summation and ultimate statement of his appeal to Middle America:

> We have among us a glib, activist element who would tell us our values are lies, and I call them impudent . . . I call them snobs for most of them disdain to mingle with the masses who work for a living . . . It has also been said that I called them intellectuals. I did not. I said that they characterized themselves as intellectuals. No true intellectual, no truly knowledgeable person, would so despise democratic institutions . . . Americans cannot afford to divide over their demagoguery—or to be deceived by their duplicity—or to let their license destroy liberty. We can, however, afford to separate them from our society—with no more regret than we should feel over discarding rotten apples from a barrel.

It had all been planned, though probably with incomplete anticipation of the response. Back in the summer, Nixon remarked to Herbert Klein, his Director of Communications, that it would be a good thing if the Vice President took a more active part than he had been playing in national politics and told Klein to publicize the increased activity. Stanley Blair, Agnew's principal assistant, presided in early September over several staff discussions of the stance that the Vice President should take. The consensus was that he should somehow try to distinguish the nation's dissidents—the unkempt young, the antiwar demonstrators, the campus rebels— from the mainstream of American opinion. And why not, while he was about it, identify them with "the liberal intellectuals" and identify that breed of gentry in turn with the leadership of the "national Democratic party"? Nobody in Agnew's service says explicitly that this was the recommended and chosen line, but it is acknowledged that the line he began to take in early October emerged from the September discussions.

At Richmond on October 2, Agnew said that "a clever liberal politician" invented the notion that Nixon had "a Southern strategy" and that "liberal pundits throughout the country leaped to exploit the catchy phrase." The "liberal wing" of "the national Democratic party" was leading it "on a runaway course to the Left." The strategy of "these new elements" was to say that America was a racist, imperialistic, warmongering nation committed to an evil war in Vietnam; to say, too, that "those who work and succeed within the traditional framework of this free nation should be ashamed of themselves, and that a good way to show regret for having been so awkward as to be successful is to support every malingerer and misfit who raises his voice in indignation." Some Virginia politicians thought at the time that this was a poor way to capture Democratic votes for Linwood Holton, the Republican candidate for Governor, but Holton won and his victory contributed to the belief that the Vice President was on a productive track. In Dallas, after avowing Nixon's dedication to the highest possible oil depletion allowance, Agnew paid his respects to "a minority of pushy youngsters and middle-aged malcontents" who think they know how "to run the world." At Montpelier, Vt., he denounced the "strident few in our society who have conferred

upon themselves a position of moral superiority" and are trying to turn the country into "a spiritual theater of the absurd."

Among the few names that illuminated Agnew's depiction of the
"liberal wing" were those of Senators J. William Fulbright and
Edmund Muskie. Agnew said that Fulbright was guilty of "ab-
solute, irresponsible nonsense" when he suggested (according to
Agnew) that the President send a representative to the funeral of
Ho Chi Minh. Muskie figured in a bizarre episode, the week after
Agnew spoke in New Orleans, that gives a fair idea of how the
Vice President functions in his more serious assays at public policy.

Agnew had resented the preoccupation of the national press and
television with his reference in New Orleans to "impudent snobs"
and the consequent failure to report the bulk of the speech, which
in the main was a standard defense of the Administration's military and domestic policies. He had dealt, among other things, with
the lack of Soviet response to the American invitation to arms
limitation talks and had said that "we would be playing Russian
roulette with US security" if the President suspended development
of multi-headed nuclear missiles. When he read after his return to
Washington that Senator Muskie had renewed his drive for such a
suspension, Agnew called in his press spokesman, Herbert Thompson, and said with some heat, "This is exactly the kind of thing I
was talking about in New Orleans." He instructed Thompson to
dig out the New Orleans text, draft from it a statement denounc-
ing Muskie, and send the statement forthwith to the Senate press
galleries. Thompson did, and Agnew was in the news with a charge
that Muskie, in "a classic example of confused thinking," was

asking the President "to play Russian roulette with U.S. security." The statement noted again that "there has been no Soviet response" to the invitation to discuss arms limitation. That was on a Wednesday. On the previous Monday, it was announced later, Ambassador Dobrynin had notified the President of the Soviet Union's readiness to open preliminary arms talks in Helsinki. The Vice president had not, in this instance, been in the state of cordial communication and coordination with the President that they are alleged to maintain.

The fact is that Nixon and Agnew have remarkably little direct communication with each other. On things that matter, such as "the subtle dangers" posed to the nation by impudent snobs and liberals "who characterize themselves as intellectuals," the President and the Vice President don't need much direct communication. They understand each other perfectly.

XXII

The Poor

The way the Nixon people tell it, Stephen Hess was at his desk in the White House basement one morning in early March, trying to think of somebody who might be fitted and willing to head up the Office of Economic Opportunity, when—like that, out of the blue, for no particular reason—the name of Congressman Donald Rumsfeld of Illinois occurred to him. Hess was President Nixon's deputy assistant for urban affairs. He and his immediate superior, Daniel P. Moynihan, had been looking for an OEO director since January. They had combed the list of the nation's college and university presidents, and had considered every Republican businessman and politician of any prominence who was known to have some social sensibility. Former Governor William Scranton of Pennsylvania had declined the honor. A retired newspaper publisher, in his sixties, a friend of the President's, had been offered the job and had then been turned aside for reasons of age. Two other prospects, a politician and a businessman, had been sounded out and had shown no interest. A simple solution, too simple for the Nixon Administration, would have been to retain Acting Director Bertrand Harding, a capable civil servant who had replaced Sargent

Shriver on a caretaker basis when he became the ambassador to Paris. But the President wanted a new man, a good Nixon Republican who could be counted upon to take the scarred and shaky OEO in hand and demonstrate that the nation's poor could be efficiently served in the Nixon style.

Rumsfeld could be that man. But would he take the job? At 36, he had been reelected in 1968 to his fourth term from a rich, nearly all-white suburban Chicago district. He had proved himself to be bright, aggressive, a hard campaigner, a fighter for reform of House procedures, a critic of OEO but a supporter of its aims. Hess had met him twice and been impressed with him, at a Harvard dinner and at the Miami Beach convention. Doubtful though he was by then that anybody would want the OEO job, more doubtful that a young Congressman with a promising career would consider it, Hess telephoned Rumsfeld at his Capitol office. To Hess's astonishment, Rumsfeld did not say no. He was soon to be off on a trip to England and the Far East, and he would think about the offer. Moynihan reported the possibility to Nixon; the President was pleased and prepared to await Rumsfeld's return although the delay in finding a director was getting to be acutely embarrassing.

On March 30, the Sunday of the Eisenhower funeral, Hess and two other White House assistants, Peter Flanigan and Harry Flemming, gave Rumsfeld the works at his modest home in the Georgetown section of Washington. The President needed him, wanted him. Mr. Nixon understood from his own experience that Rumsfeld would be giving up a secure House seat and a seemingly brilliant political future for a post that, to most politicians, would appear to be a dead end. But Nixon believed, and hoped that Rumsfeld would perceive, that with the President's backing the OEO job could open up a brighter future than Congress promised. Hess left with Rumsfeld a six-page memo, spelling it all out. Widespread doubts to the contrary notwithstanding, the President intended to retain and nurture OEO as an innovative anti-poverty instrument. Rumsfeld as its director would have Cabinet status; he would be a member of the new Urban Affairs Council; he would chair the council committee charting not only OEO's future but that of the whole poverty program.

It seemed to Rumsfeld's visitors that he was intrigued by the offer and flattered by the President's interest. But not, as yet, to the point of accepting. He fired back a memo of his own, setting forth reasons why he probably was not right for the job. He was a white Ivy Leaguer (Princeton '54), a basically conservative representative of a very conservative district, an early opponent and continuing critic of the Democratic programs administered by OEO. This said, he got to the nub: if he was really being asked to preside over the disintegration of OEO—a process which he had tried from 1964 through 1966 to bring about with votes against annual OEO authorizations—he did not want the job.

Weary of the hunt and sensing that they all but had their man, Hess and Moynihan refused to be put off. Nixon had retired to Key Biscayne in Florida for the pre-Easter season. Rumsfeld was heading for the nearby Bahamas with his friend Rogers Morton, the Maryland Congressman and new chairman of the Republican National Committee. Hess arranged for Rumsfeld to be flown to Florida in a government plane, for a secret meeting with Nixon. There the President convinced Rumsfeld that he was not, as he later said, intended to be the funeral director of OEO. In a telephone talk with Hess the next day, Rumsfeld indicated that only two hurdles remained: persuading his wife that it was the right and wise thing to do, and salary. The OEO job, then paying $30,000 a year, was soon to pay $42,500—the salary Congressmen had just begun receiving—and the Constitution could be interpreted to prevent a former Congressman from benefitting from executive raises accomplished during his elective tenure. A White House assistant who was consulted in the matter swears that he said to Rumsfeld: "Great wives respond greatly to great challenges, and fancy lawyers will figure out a way around the salary problem." Joyce Rumsfeld responded satisfactorily and John Ehrlichman, the White House Counsel, solved the salary problem. Rumsfeld would serve as OEO director without pay and draw the required $42,500 as a full assistant to the President. All concerned, the President and Rumsfeld included, promptly convinced themselves that this arrangement was further evidence of Mr. Nixon's high regard for both Rumsfeld and OEO.

No sooner was the appointment announced, with maximum emphasis upon the sacrifice Rumsfeld was making and the bright rewards foreseen by the President, than Rumsfeld's Congressional colleagues began asking him and each other why he would leave

the House of Representatives for such a job. Rumsfeld's answer—
that he welcomed a chance to work in the executive branch for a
change, and believed that he could contribute something of
value to society while doing it—rang true to a surprising number of
his friends in the House. A less kindly explanation, one that Rumsfeld calls utter rubbish, was that for all of his reputation as an up-
and-coming young politician he was really a Congressman with a
dim Congressional future and knew it. Two of his Illinois colleagues, Leslie Arends and John Anderson, stood above and ahead
of him in the House Republican leadership and there was scarcely
room in it for a third Illinois Congressman. Rumsfeld had recently
lost his one immediate chance for inclusion among his party's elite
in the House when Ohio Congressman Robert Taft, Jr. defeated
him by a single vote for the chairmanship of the Republican Research and Planning Committee. Rumsfeld had fought hard, and
with little regard for Congressional niceties, to preserve the committee against the wishes of older Republicans who look upon it
as an instrument of such young upstarts as himself, and then had
waged an equally vigorous fight for the chairmanship. He professed to take the defeat in stride, but his wife knew better. She
hand-lettered a plaque with this legend: YOU'VE WORKED
LIKE HELL, YOU'VE DONE ALL YOU CAN—AND YOU
BLEW IT! Rumsfeld hung the plaque on his office wall. He does
not deny that younger Congressmen in their third to fifth terms,

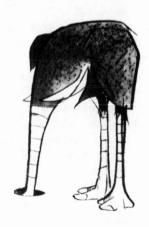

when they have got about all the place has to offer in desirable
committee assignments but still lack the seniority required for the
ultimate plums, commonly experience a frustration that drives
some to seek other work. He says that this was not what moved
him. But he recalls, discussing this aspect of Congressional life,
his decision in the 1950's, after three years as a "damn good"
Navy pilot, that he didn't want to spend the rest of his life being
"just another chauffeur."

Moderate, conservative but socially sensitive young Republicans
of Rumsfeld's Congressional generation and ilk speak of him with
sincere but expectable admiration and predict that he will make a
success of the OEO job if anybody can. For unexpected and therefore impressive testimony to the same effect, the inquirer must
turn to none other than Democratic Congressman Allard K.
Lowenstein of New York. Lowenstein, a freshman Representative
from Long Island, began working to "dump Johnson" in 1967,
when Lyndon Johnson was assumed to be undumpable. His office
on Capitol Hill is a haven for the hot-eyed young, and he himself
is a radical revolutionary by comparison with the careful and
rather staid Rumsfeld. But they have been friends and admirers of
each other since 1957, when Lowenstein was working in Washington for Hubert Humphrey and Rumsfeld for Republican Senator Robert Griffin of Michigan, then a Representative. They met
as—of all things—fellow members of an amateur wrestling club.
They once planned to buy and run a country newspaper together.
Rumsfeld offered last year to interrupt his arduous campaigning
for Nixon and campaign for Lowenstein against his Republican
opponent. Happily for Rumsfeld's relationship with Nixon, Lowenstein declined the offer.

Lowenstein recalls that in 1963, when he was working in
Mississippi to win voting rights and political muscle for Negroes,
Rumsfeld was one of the few Congressmen who was "really responsive and tried to help out." Now hear Allard Lowenstein on his
friend's promise and prospects at OEO: "I'm a fan of his. I think
he can make a great contribution to something he is interested in,
and I know he is interested, deeply interested, in doing something
about poverty in this country. . . . He is intelligent, he has in-

tegrity, he is committed. . . . I know he's going to be committed to the right things, but I'm not sure that's true of the Nixon Administration. . . . My worry is that they [at the White House] not waste him down there." Lowenstein thinks that Rumsfeld will have to broaden his concepts of what American society has to do for itself, in the way of fundamental change, before it can seriously begin to right the wrongs of the poor. But in this, too, he predicts that Rumsfeld will come up to the mark if Nixon recognizes the need and moves adequately to meet it.

A rather dubious measure of adequacy was provided in June by the Reverened Ralph David Abernathy, head of the Southern Christian Leadership Conference. He presented Nixon with demands so near to the Administration's announced and promised anti-poverty actions that Abernathy's televised complaints after the meeting sounded singularly empty. A more pertinent measure was provided by Rumsfeld's co-discoverer and sponsor, Pat Moynihan. In a speech derived from a memorandum that he prepared for the President in January and presented to the Urban Affairs Council as an initial outline of the "national urban policy" promised by Nixon, Moynihan said among other things that the federal supplement to state and city expenditures for social purposes will have to be approximately doubled (to a level that would have produced $40 billion in fiscal 1970) before true progress can be claimed. What with budgetary hold-downs to curb inflation, and a controlling estimate of the need that falls far short of Moynihan's, the Administration was a long way from an anti-poverty effort on the scale he suggested.

A Nixon appointee (not Moynihan) who was as deeply involved as anyone in the Administration with the effort to evolve a meaningful attack upon poverty and its causes was asked to skip the rhetoric and evaluate his and his companion workers' accomplishments to date. First, he said in reply, the Administration must be credited with a major effort to protect "the poor" from the impact of its counterinflationary steps. Thus, while the increase in Social Security benefits proposed by the outgoing Johnson Administration had been lowered, some increase had been recommended. The additional $300 million recommended for aid to dependent children was "very important." The Nixon proposal to free practically everybody earning incomes below official poverty

levels from federal income tax was equally significant, both for
its show of good intent and for the effect it would have if Congress
adopted it. And there was the recently declared intention, also subject to Congressional approval, to spend an additional $270
million in the next fiscal year and at least $1 billion per year
thereafter for an expanded effort to alleviate hunger.

But the biggest effort, the one consuming most of Nixon officialdom's energies and talents at this stage, was aimed at re-
vamping and improving the structures—"the systems"—through
which social reforms and advances have to be accomplished. This
took time, the Administration figured that it had the time, and (as
the President had said) it meant to take the necessary time. The
OEO, soon to be taken over by Donald Rumsfeld, was going to be
shaken up and tuned up and transformed from a marvel of scatter-
shot inefficiency into an efficient laboratory for social innovation.
(Rumsfeld, agreeing with this aim, had said rather plaintively that
experiments always produce some failures and he did hope the
public would expect and tolerate those, too.) The Johnson Model
Cities program, originally designed to concentrate urban revival in
restricted target areas, had in effect been scrapped and (at the
same estimated cost) was going to be made over into a broadened
channel for federal assistance, monetary and technical. Big things,
really big changes, were ahead for the present federal, state, and
local welfare systems. A Presidential message then in preparation
would propose the substitution of cash payments for the present
commodity and food-stamp programs; the establishment of a national minimum for welfare payments to individuals (perhaps $30
a month); and, probably though not yet certainly, direct federal
payments to supplement low earned incomes.
It was too bad (the official continued) that press and public
took so little interest in certain functional changes that had already
been accomplished or proposed. There was, for instance, the President's decision to consolidate the regional offices of federal departments and agencies (Labor, HEW, Housing and Urban
Development, OEO) with primary social responsibilities and dele-
gate more authority from Washington to them. This was dull stuff,
it also took time, but in the end it would work major improvement

in the delivery of federal services where they were intended to go and often didn't. The President had just asked Congress for authority to centralize the administration of multifarious grants for related purposes in a single agency, to be chosen by him to fit the need. The Bureau of the Budget was working out new administrative procedures, aimed at improving the allocation and delivery of planning grants and seeing to it that the recipients of such grants for similar purposes use them in similar and presumably more efficient ways.

A fair question, of course, was whether the time being taken and the energies being expended by the Nixon Administration in such structural and systemic efforts would produce results on the order and of the quality predicted for them. They might in due time add up to something worthy of being called a Nixon anti-poverty program. The Nixon approach, as those who had designed and now defended it recognized, entailed a high content of promise and a low content of specific and immediate action. Richard Nathan, one of the brighter Nixon men and the Budget Bureau's associate director "for human resources," encountered in his home a gentle touch of the impatience that he and his co-workers in the poverty field had schooled themselves to endure. Upon his return from an overnight trip to New York, he told his five-year-old daughter that he had been up there looking for better ways "to help the poor."

"That's easy, daddy," Miss Nathan said. "Just give 'em money."

XXIII

Welfare

The program of welfare reform that Mr. Nixon submitted to Congress in August was soon chewed up in the House Ways and Means Committee. The best that he could say for its prospects when he mentioned the subject on October 12 was that *"some* new approach to the whole problem of welfare" would be enacted. His staff lobbyist-in-chief, Bryce Harlow, hoped for final action in 1970 at the earliest. Others at the White House will be pleased, given the manifold skepticism and opposition evident in Congress, if the ultimate legislation represents movement "in the general direction" of the President's proposals.

Drastic revision seems so certain that only the essence of the Nixon program need be summarized here. It embodies two revolutionary principles. One is that the federal government is obligated to guarantee to welfare beneficiaries, families and individual adults, a minimum national standard of support. The other is that family heads who work for a living and earn less than a declared minimum (below "the poverty level") are entitled to a federal payment sufficient to bring their family incomes up to that minimum. A third principle, basic to the program, is not revolutionary at all.

In the opinion of many critics, including some officials who contributed importantly to the Nixon concept, it is reactionary and self-defeating. This principle is that employable beneficiaries of welfare should be made to work. If they refuse to work or to accept training for work at any job deemed by officialdom to be "suitable" for them, they (but not their dependents) should forfeit their welfare payments. Other major elements, varying from the expansion of manpower training facilities to increases in social security payments and taxes and to the assumption by the federal government of some welfare expense now borne by states and localities, figure in the total program. But the essential aspects of it, the ones that would commit the nation to a new welfare course, are the national minimum, supplementary payment to "the working poor," and the "work requirement." Whatever the outcome in Congress may be, whatever the lacks—and *The New Republic* was among the critics who found the Nixon reforms short of the need when they were announced—the welfare program reflects and constitutes the best in domestic planning and policy that we have had from the Nixon Administration.

The Nixon policy process is not likely to work in the future to better effect than it did in this instance, and it may never provide a better example of how Nixon evokes, guides, and responds to conflicting views and pressures.

One of the few genuine convictions that Nixon brought to his Presidency and stuck to through the initial months was that the welfare system was an "utter disaster" and required fundamental change. His campaign chatter about getting dependent millions "off welfare rolls and onto payrolls" obscured a more sophisticated understanding that it was not really, as so much of his rhetoric suggested, a simple matter of putting the bums to work. A task force headed by Richard Nathan of the Brookings Institution, now an associate director of the Budget Bureau, came up with the main lines of the President's eventual approach before he was elected. His White House assistant for urban affairs, Daniel P. Moynihan, won that appointment and Nixon's confidence in part with some informed and strongly asserted views of how welfare change should be accomplished. Thus fortified by expertise, Nixon first promised to produce a complete welfare program in March. But he discovered in that month that even the proposal of welfare reform required the resolution of basic conflicts between his own experts, between members of his Cabinet, between *their* experts, and—more fundamentally—between an inevitable rise in welfare costs and the President's competing commitment to hold down the federal budget.

The personal alignments among those advising the President were soon fairly clear, though never as simple as many "inside" accounts indicated. One of the polar figures was Arthur Burns, an economist who during the Eisenhower Administration, earned national distinction and Nixon's trust. As Nixon's White House Counsellor, the only assistant with Cabinet status, Burns was nominally responsible for the formulation of all domestic programs. He left the White House in early 1970 to be chairman of the Federal Reserve Board. But his standing with and influence upon Nixon continue, and he powerfully affected the slow evolution of the welfare program. His rather ponderous and relentless harping upon costs forced successive estimates of new federal expenditures for the Nixon changes up to $4.4 billion, a figure that was revised upward later on and, when submitted, was at least a billion short of the real costs. One facet of Burns' role would have been comical if it had concerned less serious a matter. The ebullient Moynihan, HEW Secretary Robert Finch, Labor Secretary George Shultz, and other advocates of the most generous and humane approach attainable within foreseeable budgetary limits were under the impression, well into July, that they were getting somewhere in their insistence to Nixon that the "work requirement" wanted by Burns was mistaken in principle and would be impossible to administer in practice. Nixon had agreed in private with Burns, months earlier, that a strong work requirement would be written firmly into the final recommendations. Knowing this, Burns accepted with more equanimity than he chose to display in council the proposal to extend supplementary income support to the "working poor"—a concept, hitherto alien to his conservative mind, that he actually but never openly came to applaud in principle and did not resist when the chips were down.

Another influential and, in this affair, somewhat misunderstood adviser was Attorney General John N. Mitchell. A natural assumption, in view of his cramped social attitudes in general, was that he would oppose to the end a national welfare minimum that

overrode state standards. The proposal to supplement earnings of
the "working poor" with federal money might have been expected
to send him up the walls of Nixon's Oval Office. Mitchell sat with
Nixon and the others concerned in uncounted Cabinet, Cabinet
Economic Committee, Urban Affairs Council, and UAC sub-com-
mittee meetings devoted to the evolving welfare program. Never
once, according to officials at those meetings, was he heard to open
his mouth on the subject. He expressed himself only to Nixon, in
private. But two impressions prevail and are taken as fact by the
others. The first is that he early recognized and settled for Nixon's
determination to bring about real welfare change. The second
impression is that he came down in the end, in late July and early
August, on the side of the relatively liberal approach fought for
by Moynihan, Shultz, Finch, and Nixon's anti-poverty director,
ex-Congressman Donald Rumsfeld of Illinois.

In June, impatient to get along with the business and sensitive
to the view that he was proving to be a domestic laggard, Nixon
took the responsibility for staff coordination away from Moynihan
and Burns, who were opposed on every major welfare issue, and
assigned it to Counsel John Ehrlichman. In order to give Ehrlichman and his helpers something coherent to work with, Secretary
Shultz was instructed to synthesize the competing alternatives in
a single paper. The resulting document was notable for two things
—its cavalier dismissal of Burns' cherished work requirement, and
a recommended standard of federal payments to both the working
poor and to the wholly dependent poor that considerably exceeded
the modest levels recommended to Congress by Nixon. Shultz
functioned at this stage as an analyst of others' views and as an
advocate of his own. Ehrlichman professed to the advisers whom
he was coordinating that he intruded no views of his own. But he
had views, he expressed them to Nixon, and they (like Mitchell's)
served on balance to favor the Moynihan-Shultz-Finch approach
over the cautious policy that Burns continued to urge upon the
President.

By the time Nixon took off on his Asian tour in July, he had
made his basic welfare decisions and had imparted them to Ehrlichman, who shaped them up in a semi-final discussion draft which

he delivered to the President in Bucharest. Nixon and Ehrlichman refined the draft in talks aboard Air Force One, during the last legs of the homeward flight, and the Administration's welfare program was to all effects complete when the President landed.

On August 6, two days before he presented the program in somewhat oversimple terms to the country on television, and three days before he departed Washington for a month in California, Nixon summoned the Cabinet, Vice President Agnew, and the staff assistants principally concerned with developing the proposals to the Presidential retreat at Camp David, Md. His purpose, Nixon said in opening the all-day session, was to tell those present what he had decided. He said that the decisions were firm and would not be changed. But he wanted to hear, surely not for the first time in most instances, what his associates and subordinates thought about the decisions. He could have been implying, though some who were there were not entirely sure that this was intended, that those who opposed the decided program in part or altogether should say so then and be silent thereafter.

It was soon reported that only three Cabinet members—Finch, Shultz and Rumsfeld (who had Cabinet rank)—spoke up in support of the whole program. A more meaningful fact was that Mitchell and Defense Secretary Melvin Laird did not speak against it. Laird had been the ranking Republican member of the House Appropriations Subcommittee dealing with welfare, he was regarded by the President and others as an authority on the subject, and his opposition to the adopted approach during the period when it was evolving could have been decisive. His demeanor of acceptance at the Camp David meeting indicated that he never had opposed it. George Romney, the Secretary of Housing and Urban Development, didn't like it—he preferred reliance upon his department's Model Cities approach to urban problems—and he said so in his rough and evangelical way. Burns and Secretary of the Treasury Kennedy restated, mildly, their known doubts that the prospective costs had been adequately calculated and weighed. But the star performer, in more ways than one, was Vice President Agnew. He said that he deplored and abhorred the extension of welfare rights and support to the working poor. He saw no saving merit in the claim, soon to be emphasized by Nixon, that the work requirement kept the program from guaranteeing an income, however low, to everybody who qualified for welfare, regardless of whether they were too lazy to work. Men there who thought him utterly wrong said afterward that Agnew spoke with passion and dignity. He stated his views at a mid-day luncheon and then left to preside over the Senate. The manner of his leaving will not be forgotten.

The Senate was about to vote on Nixon's Safeguard anti-ballistic missile system, the issue was close, and the President counted on Agnew to cast the deciding vote for Safeguard if there was a tie. Agnew turned at the door of the lunchroom and said to Nixon, "Mr. President, if there is a tie I may telephone you before I vote and ask you whether you've changed your mind about this welfare program."

———

Prospects for enactment of the Nixon welfare reforms appeared to be improving in early 1970.

XXIV

Moynihan at Work

At a meeting of the new Council for Urban Affairs on March 6, President Nixon told his assistant for urban affairs, Daniel Patrick Moynihan, who is also the Council's executive secretary, to get to work right away on a written appraisal of the Council's performance to date. Had it proved to be really useful and, if so, in what ways? Were the President, the other Council members, Moynihan himself and his staff of assistant assistants on the right track in their attempt to develop the "national urban policy" that Mr. Nixon called for when he established the Council by executive order on his third day in office?

These were good questions. The Council and its nine sub-councils were great consumers of high-level executive time. Nixon presided at six of the first eight Council sessions, spending one and one-half to three hours at each of them. Vice President Agnew and the seven Cabinet members who are Council members as well understood that their attendance at its meetings was all but mandatory. (HEW Secretary Robert H. Finch begged off like a truant schoolboy from the March 6 meeting, explaining that he could hardly offend powerful Congressmen by cancelling a previously

A fine
broth of a boy!

scheduled and conflicting committee appearance.) The President's busy Counsellor, Arthur F. Burns, and Richard Nathan, the Budget Bureau's Associate Director for Human Resources, were at every session in the White House Cabinet Room. They and their staffs, in effect backing up Moynihan's small staff, devoted uncounted working hours to preparing items for discussion by the Council and to studies ordered by it and the President. Under secretaries and assistant secretaries of the departments and department staffers assigned to the work of the sub-councils added to the immense amount of time and labor committed to "urban affairs" and the early effort to demonstrate that the vast range of social problems encompassed in that term could be more intelligently defined and better handled by this Administration than they had been in the past.

Moynihan delegated the preparation of answers to the President's questions to Stephen Hess, his principal deputy, and to his staff counsel, John Price. Their responding memorandum and Moynihan's report to the President must be judged with some understanding of the atmosphere of the Nixon White House—earnest, trite in the favored modes of expression, but not to be sneered at because of that. The Moynihan staff felt, the President was told, that "the Council has been successful in providing a Presidential perspective to its members." It was worthwhile, indeed essential, that the Attorney General and the six Cabinet secretaries on the Council view the urban problem as the President viewed it, and that they have occasion at the Council meetings to see its many facets from his White House pinnacle rather than always from their own departmental crannies. The Council and the sub-councils, to one or more of which all the Cabinet-ranking members belonged, also enabled each of them to perceive the issues before them in the same terms—a point highly valued by Moynihan, who holds it to be the beginning and the essence of practicable solutions to diverse and complex social problems. A means of providing such a common view was what he had in mind when he recommended the establishment of the Urban Council to the President, and after six weeks of trial he was prepared to argue that it had already fulfilled the purpose.

How to state another justifying point with becoming modesty was something of a problem in itself, but one that Moynihan and his helpers could be counted upon to solve. Their point was that the Council had provided a useful forum for Daniel Patrick Moynihan and for the instruction that he variously volunteered and was called upon to give the President, the Vice President, and the other Council members. At one of the first meetings, he presented and explained at length a paper that could, according to his associates, be taken as at least the basis of "a national urban policy." It ranged from large abstractions to such specifics as the need to provide federal incentives for performance as well as for planning in Model Cities programs and to require, as a condition for continued federal funding, higher levels of management and performance in subsidized state and local agencies than had usually been demanded. On another occasion, at Nixon's request, Moynihan undertook to explain why it is that in recent years the numbers of people on welfare rolls have risen astronomically while the numbers of employed increased, instead of declining with the declines in the totals of unemployed. "I came up with a theory about it," he said, refusing to elaborate.

This disquisition was one of four items on the agenda of the March 6 meeting, which was described as an example of the Council at its talkative best. Moynihan's analysis of the welfare-employment phenomenon sparked a discussion that ranged from the pros and cons of a higher minimum wage to restrictive labor practices in the construction industry, the social uses of birth control, and the persisting migration of poor Americans from the countryside to the cities. Deputy Defense Secretary David Packard and a supporting Pentagon team reported on the status of efforts, initiated by former Secretaries McNamara and Clifford and neglected until then by Secretary Melvin Laird, to infuse some broad social objectives and benefits into defense recruiting, training, housing, and other activities. The President displayed great interest in the subject and gave others present the impression that he meant to jack up Secretary Laird and see to it that these recently lagging elements in the defense effort were vigorously supported. A report on summer youth programs for the urban poor held that they were badly conceived and organized and could stand much improvement. But the programs for the summer of 1969 had already been approved and funded, there would be no point in knocking them, so the best thing to do—the President and Vice

President Agnew declared—was to shelve the proffered report, keep quiet, and begin steps to reorganize and improve the summer programs for subsequent years. George Romney, the Secretary of Housing and Urban Development, had brought for discussion a draft of a statement on his cherished plans to enlist voluntary institutions in the overall urban and poverty programs. But time was running out, the President had to leave and Romney was told to save his paper for the next meeting.

At that point, only two tangible results had emerged from the Council and the Moynihan shop. An Office of Minority Business Enterprise had been established in the Department of Commerce, under the supervision of Secretary Maurice Stans, with orders to make a reality of candidate Nixon's talk about "black capitalism" by coordinating and stimulating the 116 separate federal programs aimed at helping black and other minority Americans to found, finance, and manage their own businesses. It was hit upon as a way of demonstrating serious intent without additional cost, and in terms of the numbers of people benefited, its accomplishments could be no more than marginal.

Parts of four Council sessions, five meetings of a sub-council headed by Secretary Finch, hundreds of staff hours and several office sessions with the President produced his February 19 message to Congress, in which he promised to deliver before June 30 a definitive statement of his anti-poverty philosophy and program and in the meantime undertook to retain in modified form the Johnson Administration's central anti-poverty instrument, the Office of Economic Opportunity. It was the decision to maintain OEO rather than the interim delegation of OEO's Head Start program for preschool children to the Department of Health, Education, and Welfare, and of the Job Corps (which Nixon had promised to abolish) to the Department of Labor, that gave some indication of the Nixon Administration's approach to the poverty problem. It was only an indication, but on its face it justified Moynihan's claim on behalf of the President that it constituted a believable commitment. In this sense, and with the reservation that it was yet to be implemented by meaningful action, it was in contrast to Nixon's raucous campaign chatter about moving people

"off the welfare rolls and onto payrolls" and shifting the burden of alleviating American poverty from the national government to private enterprise, the states, and localities. A strong belief in the capacity of nonfederal instruments to share the burden persisted and was soon to be expressed in a spate of Council and staff recommendations and executive actions. But, more convincingly than he did during his campaign, Nixon in office had acknowledged the basic federal responsibility for treating national and urban ills.

Moynihan was credited at the White House with a good deal of responsibility for this shift in tone and also for the tactical caution that marked the Nixon approach. The decision at the March 6 Council meeting to avoid both criticsm and explicit defense of the summer youth program was typical. The President's OEO message to Congress was framed in part to anticipate and offset two studies of anti-poverty programs. A summary report on the whole anti-poverty effort, ordered by Congress last year, was about to be released by the General Accounting Office, with case studies of 50 anti-poverty projects around the country to follow. The GAO's examples of mismanagement, bumbling, and plain thievery were expected to get the headlines and obscure what White House and other officials with advance knowledge of the report considered to be the constructive suggestions for reform also included in it. A report on the Head Start preschool program, prepared for OEO by the Westinghouse Learning Corporation, emphasized its failings, particularly the evidence that its effects on black and other deprived children fade away once they enter the public schools. The Administration braced itself to argue that this was a challenge to improve both Head Start and the schools rather than an invitation to scrap the effort.

Moynihan went about his work in his pleasant office in the West Wing basement with his usual zest. Whether his small staff of young enthusiasts, which he managed as he would a seminar of friends, was big enough to handle his many spot assignments and still do the long-range planning also intended was a question that he refused to face. His deputy, Stephen Hess, called in an experienced government administrator to study the setup and eventually confronted Moynihan with a recommendation, instantly rejected, that he either enlarge the staff or reduce the load that he put upon it and himself. Personal preferences apart, Moynihan has a sound theory that big staffs are more likely than small staffs to try to take command of the programs and departments with which they work.

Moynihan spent a lot of time with Nixon in the early months, usually with others rather than alone with the President. "The poor fellow," Moynihan said, "is seldom more than three hours away from another meeting with me." He maintained that Nixon in private was not the dry stick that some others find him to be and that he enjoyed the famous Moynihan wit. A cited example was well below Moynihan's par and close to Nixon's par. As the March 6 meeting of the Urban Council was breaking up, the matter of appointing women to responsible jobs arose. Nixon jokingly asked Moynihan how many women he had on his staff (answer: none). "Mr. President," Moynihan said, "I am forbidden by the Civil Rights Act of 1964 to inquire whether the members of my staff are male or female." Nixon laughed.

XXV

Where is Pat?

In a commencement address at the University of Rochester in 1966, Richard Nixon said: "Woodrow Wilson's distinction between men of thought and men of action can no longer be made. The man of thought who will not act is ineffective; the man of action who will not think is dangerous." William Safire, then as now a Nixon speech writer, recalls that he and Mr. Nixon sweated for hours over that passage. It seemed to Safire that Nixon was insistent that the chosen language say exactly what he meant because it expressed something very important to him in his estimation of himself. The President considers himself to be a man of thought *and* action, and he wants and needs to have around him, at his instant call and total disposal, other men to whom he attributes the dual quality that he perceives and values in himself.

Mr. Nixon evidently believes that he has two such men in the persons of Daniel P. Moynihan and Bryce N. Harlow, former White House assistants who have been retitled "Counsellors to the President" and given Cabinet rank. When the President announced and explained this and other steps in a reorganization of the White House staff to his assembled Cabinet, he said that

Moynihan and Harlow were to be "ministers without portfolio," in the British style. They were present and, although they professed to have no qualms about their new status and duties, I suspect that they cringed just a little, inwardly, when the President spoke in that way of his new Counsellors. Harlow's experience in government dates back to 1938, Moynihan's to the Kennedy Administration, and they must know that "ministers without portfolio" are likely to find themselves in the unhappy position of corporate vice presidents on detached duty, favored with exerything except the authority to accomplish whatever they are supposed to get done. Any suggestion to this effect at the White House brings the response that it indicates a basic misunderstanding of the Nixon establishment and of the President who heads it. Maybe so, but both Harlow and Moynihan have a lively awareness of the perils that could await them as Mr. Nixon's in-house philosophers unless they retain some areas of specific authority.

The announcement of the staff reorganization said that Harlow, who had been the Assistant for Congressional Relations, "will continue policy guidance of congressional relations," and Harlow said for himself that "I am to maintain policy oversight in this area." Moynihan, hitherto the Assistant for Urban Affairs and executive secretary of the Urban Affairs Council, was to "continue his policy guidance in urban problems." A new Assistant for Congressional Relations and an Urban Council executive secretary (but not another Assistant for Urban Affairs) were to be appointed. They were to be pitied, for they were certain to be overshadowed as well as overseen by their predecessors. Harlow in his field of legislative expertise and Moynihan in the whole sweep of social concerns, will continue to be either the President's top men or nobodies, and neither is the nobody type.

Pat Moynihan is a certified liberal Democrat, the only figure at anywhere near the Nixon peaks who qualifies for that description. He is a thinker, an innovator, a strong advocate of his own views, a witty and passionate man who knows how to please the President with his humor and, one must judge from the favor shown him, also knows how to keep his passion within the bounds that Mr. Nixon is prepared to tolerate. A good many of his

White House associates and perhaps Moynihan himself regret the departure from the President's staff of the first and until recently the only Counsellor to the President, Arthur Burns, a conservative economist who was appointed chairman of the Federal Reserve Board. A pronounced tension, personal and philosophical, quickly developed between Burns and Moynihan, and in the opinion of others who worked with them it contributed materially to the range and worth of the policy choices that were presented to the President.

Bryce Harlow, Moynihan's fellow Counsellor, is also a deeply conservative man, but not a philosophical conservative in the sense

that Arthur Burns is. Harlow's conservatism—and this is said with respect—is that of a political technician, valued by the President for (among other talents) his skill at spotting what he calls "the land-mines" that may be buried in some otherwise laudable policy proposal or program. His largest or anyhow his most obvious service to Nixon, as it was in times past to Dwight Eisenhower, has been to forewarn the President of possible dangers, of likely and avoidable opposition, and to tailor both the expressions and the content of policy in ways calculated to avert or minimize the opposition. Considering the extent of unexpected congressional opposition that Nixon encountered in matters ranging from his ABM system to the Haynsworth nomination, Harlow's reputation in this respect seemed to some people to have been substantially impaired. But it obviously was not impaired at the White House and with the President. Harlow's associates generally expected him to be more of a cautionary than a creative Counsellor. They also expected him to provide a certain counterpoint to the more adventurous Moynihan. It happens that Harlow stands 5 feet 4 inches, Moynihan 6 feet 5 inches, a circumstance that led a junior Nixon assistant to remark that in any confrontation they will face each other " eyeball to knee-cap."

Moynihan said that he was freed from detailed responsibilities so that he could be available to Nixon "for counselling of one kind and another on a fairly wide range of subjects." Harlow said that his and Moynihan's concerns as Counsellors may stretch "from here to infinity, in an expanding universe," and he included in his own range of possible advice the problems of Vietnam, world peace, inflation, law and order, and governmental reform. A simpler statement of their point is that Nixon likes to chew the fat with both of them, on any subject that may come up, and that his first purpose in granting them their new status and freedom was to have them at hand for that exercise whenever he finds time for it. Never mind that Moynihan lately has spent a lot of his time on the road, defending the Administration's social policies and vision and promising bold advances to come, and that he went off to Europe in December to encourage joint NATO efforts toward social betterment. I am assured that what Nixon wanted from Moynihan was Moynihan, in person. "Are we tracking with Pat?" Nixon asked an assistant after the staff changes were announced. "Where is he? I want to see him." The President did, soon afterward, in private and in group meetings, for seven hours straight.

White House skeptics asked each other, "Where is Pat?" in a tone of suspicion that Moynihan was on or headed toward a splendidly upholstered shelf. A staff of young and innovative Republicans that he built for the Urban Affairs Council was dismantled and most of its members were reassigned to John Ehrlichman, the Assistant for Domestic Affairs. Moynihan had permission to recruit "a couple of youngsters" for a reduced staff of his own, but for major assistance he had to look thereafter to the expanded Ehrlichman staff. None of this seemed to bother him, and perhaps it shouldn't have, but it bothered some of those among his White House associates who considered that anything that appeared to diminish Moynihan diminished the Administration.

A question not discussed at the White House, unless an outsider brought it up, was whether Pat Moynihan could continue to be comfortable with the Nixon who let Vice President Spiro T. Agnew speak for him and the Administration in the way that Agnew was speaking in late 1969. Agnew's call to the mob—and that was what it was—for support of the President in Vietnam and, by extension, in domestic matters as well should have discomfited Moynihan and at least a few others at the Nixon White House. There was, at the time, no indication that it did, except in the most minor fashion. Moynihan said on November 17 that the Agnew line did not disturb him. He expected to be around as long as he found himself free to speak his mind to the President as he had been up to then, and free also to speak for the Administration in his own field of social equity. At this writing, that is where Pat is. I am not as confident as Moynihan professes to be that he will be there indefinitely.

XXVI

Thought for Food

A week before the White House Conference on Food, Nutrition and Health was to open in Washington, nobody at the White House could tell President Nixon just how many people he was likely to be addressing on the morning of December 2 or guarantee to the Secret Service that he would not be booed, cursed, and generally maligned by some of his hearers. Professor Jean Mayer, a Harvard nutritionist who had been organizing the conference for the President since mid-June and, in the process, acquiring an education in political and social realities that he'd never thought he needed, hoped to hold the attendance to some 2600 academics, corporation executives, blacks, Indians, feminists, Pacific islanders, students, Mexican-Americans, congressmen, and members of organizations varying from the American Legion and the US Chamber of Commerce to the Appalachian Volunteers and Mississippi's Delta Foundation.

At least twice that many people had demanded the right to attend. Among the invited and the uninvited there were some who were determined that the conference should not be the three-day exercise in peaceful, constructive contribution to the Nixon

Administration's proclaimed purposes to end hunger and malnutrition in the United States "for all time" that Professor Mayer and his Presidential associates envisaged. Walter Washington, the District of Columbia's black mayor, had arranged to have the luxury hotel that had been preempted for the conference thoroughly but unobtrusively policed. The mayor's policemen had orders to seize and eject any malcontents who might try to disrupt the plenary sessions or the 20-plus group sessions at which the serious work of the conference was to be done. The preliminaries proved, if nothing else, that hunger in America and the less spectacular ills of malnutrition had come to constitute a true national cause. It had become both imperative and politically profitable for Mr. Nixon to fulfill his promise that the conference findings "will be the basis for action by this Administration and the beginning of a national commitment—to put an end to malnutrition and hunger among the poor, to make better use of our agricultural bounty and nutritional knowledge, and to ensure a healthful diet for all Americans."

The President had little notion of what he was getting into last May when he projected the conference as an affair for "executives from the nation's leading food processing and food distribution companies and trade unions" who would advise him on how to improve government food programs and inspire "the private food market . . . to improve the nutritional status of all Americans." That undertaking was part of a hasty effort, in response to belatedly recognized Congressional pressures, to come up with a convincing Presidential message on "Hunger in America" and, specifically, to beef up the Administration's parsimonious allocation of funds in the current (fiscal 1970) budget for food stamps for the hungry poor. Nixon ordered his Budget Bureau to squeeze an extra $270 million for food stamps out of defense estimates, and the Senate and House eventually authorized and appropriated $610 million. Since the $610 million was to be spent in the remaining half of fiscal 1970, it established an annual level of $1.2 billion for food-stamp assistance and rendered the Nixon claim of "a total program of $2.5 billion" for the alleviation of hunger more credible than it previously was.

A White House figure who did know what the President was getting into was his urban affairs specialist, Daniel Patrick Moynihan. Given the President's commitment to a hunger conference, Moynihan immediately set about broadening its scope and invited Jean Mayer to accept the temporary title of Special Consultant in charge of organizing it. The first of the results, in the forms of 26 surprisingly positive and innovative panel reports on every conceivable aspect of the hunger problem were in hand before the conference opened. Whatever else may be said about this conference, and in my opinion it proved to be a useful stimulant to federal action, it contributed enormously to the instruction of one American, French-born Professor Mayer, in the ways and

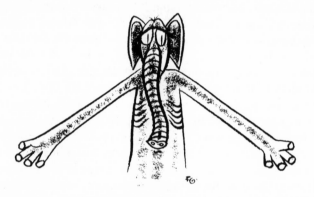

turmoils of the body politic and also of the curious institution at its apex, the Nixon White House.

Mayer was anything but an isolated academician when he moved from Cambridge to the White House in June. Long before hunger was a cause for anyone except the few zealots who were really aware of its extent in America, it and the related problems of dietary deficiencies were his causes. He was the first witness called by Senator George McGovern's select committee on hunger. He had a hand in launching the Citizens Inquiry and the CBS television documentary, "Hunger in America," that in 1967–68 did much to force the problem to national attention. He was a founder and the first chairman of the aggressive National Council on Hunger and Malnutrition, a private organization dedicated to making the well-fed so uncomfortable about the unfed and ill-fed that they will support or at least tolerate the national expenditure of money and effort that is necessary if all Americans are to be adequately fed. Professor Mayer thought, in short, that he knew the score and expected serious opposition and hindrance only from entrenched conservatives, in Congress and in business, when he took on the conference job. He was in for a shock, and he got it from unexpected quarters.

He discovered, first of all, that the Nixon establishment had given no practical thought to the matter of financing the conference. How to meet his budget of $950,000 was still a problem for him when the conference opened. Travel and living expenses had to be provided for at least half the conference participants, including several hundred representatives of "the poor." Mayer extracted $250,000 from the Department of Health, Education, and Welfare, wangled $500,000 from the Ford, Rockefeller, and Kellogg Foundations (the latter, he takes care to say, no relation to Kellogg Foods), and looked to the Office of Economic Opportunity and the Agriculture Department for $200,000. Legal obstacles to the OEO and Agriculture contributions had not been foreseen, and some of the money never was put up.

Mayer's own National Council was a source of pain and trouble. Its executive director, Washington attorney John R. Kramer (who had been hired by Mayer), expressed a suspicion in one of its publications that the White House conference would turn out to be "a quasi-academic research and study session . . . not vitally concerned with producing substantial increments of social change" and that "the poor and the consumers" invited to it would be submerged and undone by "professors and businessmen." Kramer kept and shared with any journalists who asked him for it a discouraging tally of Administration actions on hunger matters to date, a summary of niggardly budgetary positions that on its face brought into question the President's promise of a genuine "national commitment." It seemed to Mayer that staff members in the service of Senator McGovern and other congressional hunger-fighters sniped at him and his efforts, planting press reports (false, Mayer says) that the White House required political clearance for participants in the conference and insisted that the roles of black and other minority militants be kept to a manageable minimum. The counter-effect, Mayer says, was to arouse distrust

among those same militants, thereby impeding efforts to bring a
representative cross-section of them into the conference. This kind
of fire from theoretically friendly quarters convinced Mayer that
too many people in the anti-hunger ranks want to preserve the
problem as a partisan issue, and that too many others see in it
"a symbolic issue" to be used more to further their own prescrip-
tions for social reform than to abolish hunger and malnutrition.

The force of these and kindred plaints at the White House was
reduced by the acknowledged truth of a story involving Senator
McGovern. Jean Mayer, who continued to regard the Senator
as a friend of the conference, asked him in July if he would be
willing to address it if he were formally invited. McGovern said
that he would be happy to. McGovern was told in October that
he would not be invited to speak. Mayer later explained: "The
fact that Senator McGovern is considered to be a leading candidate for the Presidency on the Democratic side seems to us to
be a good reason to get a different Senator." Another Democrat,
Walter Mondale of Minnesota, was chosen. Professor Mayer may
like to know that John Kramer of the National Council immediately went to work on a draft of Senator Mondale's conference speech.

XXVII

Dr. King's Memorial

Mrs. Coretta King, up from Atlanta and in New York to celebrate the publication of her gentle and loving memoir, *My Life with Martin Luther King, Jr.,* says that President Nixon's "indifferent attitude" has doomed her proposal that the federal government sponsor and create a national park in her assassinated husband's honor in downtown Atlanta. She adds that her experience with Mr. Nixon "suggests that he has not evolved from racist reflexes." In view of the Nixon Administration's record of minimal action and continuous equivocation in every field having to do with minority and civil rights, and of the President's past and continuing appeal to the Southern white vote, the charge is believable. But inquiry suggests that the story is not that simple. What we have here, on the Administration side, is the plight of men of good will—and the President *has* demonstrated good will in this matter—who have, by other actions, engulfed themselves in a kind of moral twilight. On the other side, Mrs. King's side, we have a demonstration that easy judgments, easy attributions of every denial of the hopes and proposals of black individuals, groups, and leaders to "racist reflexes" are no longer as acceptable as they once were.

A foundation to bring into being an appropriate memorial to Dr. King was established soon after he was shot dead in Memphis on April 4, 1968. On its boards of directors and trustees are Mrs. King, former Vice President Hubert Humphrey, Senators Hugh Scott of Pennsylvania and Edward Kennedy, and Dr. King's successor at the head of the Southern Christian Leadership Conference, the Reverend Ralph David Abernathy. Its attorney is Harry Wachtel of New York, a friend of the King family and a source of some of the information given here.

The proposal discussed with the Nixon Administration was first submitted to President Johnson in July of 1968. He referred it to then Vice President Humphrey. Its central feature was and is that the incumbent President ask Congress for authority to condemn and purchase approximately 15 acres in downtown Atlanta —not merely "the two downtown blocks" mentioned in an interview with Mrs. King in *The New York Times*—and maintain the site as a national park. It encompasses Dr. King's birthplace, the church where he preached and his father still preaches, several businesses and many dwellings, and a Catholic church. All of the structures except the King birthplace and church would have to be demolished or removed. A memorial tomb, a library, an Institute for Advanced Afro-American Studies, possibly a center for black social action, would be built on the site with federal and private funds. What was asked of Mr. Johnson and later of Mr. Nixon was, above all, Presidential sponsorship of the whole enterprise, to be symbolized and made real by federal acquisition and maintenance of a *national* park.

Harry McPherson, a Johnson assistant, and a member of the Humphrey staff, along with several agency officials, reviewed the proposal and discussed it with Wachtel through the summer and fall of '68. Partly because of a feeling, shared by Wachtel, that Humphrey's nomination and candidacy for the Presidency would give approval at that time an unwanted partisan tinge, it was tacitly agreed that action should be delayed until the next Presi-

dent took office. Mrs. King discussed the proposal by telephone
with President Nixon in early February and, she says, found him
sympathetic. He assigned the matter to Leonard Garment, a former
law partner who had just been transferred to the firm's Washington office and who later joined the White House staff. Garment's
credentials as a concerned libertarian are unassailable. Wachtel
says that throughout his and Garment's subsequent discussions
"Leonard Garment and I had a very good relationship. I found
him to be a sympathetic man."

But it seemed to Wachtel from early April onward that "the
position he had to take raised some questions." The questions
raised were of the kind suggested by Mrs. King in her reference
to "racist reflexes." Leonard Garment says that the position he
took was his own—in essence, that the national park and "the
architectural memorial" proposed by Mrs. King and the King
Foundation were not "appropriate"; that Presidential and federal
acceptance and sponsorship of such a memorial "would not be
the right thing to do." In a talk with Mrs. King in Atlanta on
April 3, and in a letter to her in July, HEW Secretary Robert
Finch agreed with Garment that federal contributions to and
other help with "a living memorial" of the kind represented by
the proposed Afro-American Institute would be "suitable." At
Garment's suggestion, Nixon in May authorized the National

Park Service to landscape and maintain, indefinitely, any memorial park acreage that might be acquired by the city of Atlanta (which pleaded poverty) or with private funds. At Nixon's order, HEW and George Romney's Department of Housing and Urban Development, among other agencies, scrounged for and identified funds that might supplement a private memorial endeavor. That was as far as the President would go, and Garment so wrote Mrs. King on August 1.

There were unacknowledged considerations. What remains of the nation's fragmented "black leadership" kept remarkably silent. Ralph Abernathy, occupied since Dr. King's murder with establishing his own leadership, publicly asked prospective donors to give their money to SCLC and not to earmark it for the memorial. The Nixon staff knew that certain Southern congressmen possessed and were all too ready to produce records of the kind hinted at by a television panelist who asked Mrs. King: "Were you ever aware that at least certain agents of the FBI were spreading scurrilous stories about your husband among newsmen and others?" She replied, obliquely and sadly, that she was.

There the matter rested. On the Monday after Mrs. King voiced her complaint and suspicions, Dr. Vincent Harding of the King Foundation staff discussed the continuing possibility of federal supplementation of private funds with an HEW official in Washington. Garment, HEW, HUD, and other agencies remained under the President's order to do all they could for the memorial, short of acquiring and sustaining a national park in honor of Martin Luther King.

XXVIII

Europe in the "New Era"

That absurd device of government and journalism, the "high official" who can never be quoted by name, is sometimes invented by reporters who have been in contact with nobody higher in rank than a press officer. But there are occasions, and President Nixon's trip to Europe in February was one of them, when the high official really does exist, either illuminating or befogging large events with statements that may not be charged then or later to the individual who made them, and so guarding himself or his master, in this case the President, against any embarrassment that may result from assertions that turn out to have been injudicious, mistaken or deliberately misleading.

Home from Europe after a week of exposure there to the high officials who accompanied Mr. Nixon and spoke for him when he was not speaking for himself, I have been looking over my notes of their remarks. This may seem to be a back-door way of reviewing the Nixon trip, but it is not. The intent of the anonymous spokesmen was to clarify what the President said publicly, to explain what he was really up to, and to assess the results of his efforts in terms assumed to be more realistic, because privately stated, than those offered by the President in Europe and in Washington afterward at a televised press conference. What his high officials said on his behalf seems in retrospect to have been neither injudicious, probably mistaken nor deliberately misleading. It was mostly so near in effect to what he said publicly that they might as well have talked for quotation.

Yet there is about their explanations and assessments a certain unreality, as if they had been talking about a Europe that exists principally in their and their President's minds and hopes. It is, these spokesmen seem to have been saying, a Europe that is at once intimately entwined with the United States and perfectly entitled to make its own arrangements for dealing amongst its own governments and with the United States, without much if any regard for the preferences and interests of the United States. It also is, the President seems to have been saying through his high officials, a Europe with which the United States has been too much engaged and too little concerned in recent times; a Europe from which the United States now should and can disengage to an important extent; but also a Europe, the same Europe, for which the United States should assert, and in the person of Mr. Nixon is asserting, a deeper and more genuine and more intelligently implemented concern than the preceding Administrations displayed.

To those who detect in all this some confusion of definition and purpose, a note of contradiction, the high officials speaking for Mr. Nixon reply that, in a phrase heard several times along the Nixon route, the skeptical must understand that we are in "a new era." It is, we of the press were told, the era brought into being on January 20 with the Inauguration of President Nixon. How, personalities apart, does it differ in fundamental circumstances from the eras of John Kennedy and Lyndon Johnson? The answer seriously and responsibly offered went as follows: First, the United States is now committed to "a reasonable settlement" in Vietnam. Second, it is seeking a settlement of the Middle-East conflict between Israel and its Arab enemies "without war." Third and emphatically, the United States now is not only "willing" to negotiate the major issues that divide it and the Soviet Union but is preparing an "approach" to negotiation and a program for it that is "serious, complete, and detailed." And fourth, it is expressing these aims and preparing to accomplish them through processes of communication and consultation with its European allies that are more open, more effective, less clogged with extraneous incidentals and invective than those that have inhibited or in some instances blocked communication with Europe in the eras now happily ended.

The purpose of the foregoing is neither to minimize Nixon's performance in Europe—it was quite impressive—nor to suggest, as columnist Joseph Kraft did from London, that the journey accomplished nothing of value. One of the President's exalted explainers observed in perhaps the wisest judgment that came from them, that only subsequent events will make a sound appraisal possible. Presumably in full knowledge that he was doing so, the President put himself at the mercy of the European leaders whom he visited and lauded. General de Gaulle, for instance, could embarrass his late guest with another disruptive whack at the Western system if he inflicts it soon after being praised for possessing in marvelous degree "the quality of wisdom and vision . . . the perspective that leaders need to make the right decisions." Circumstances and the French public could have the same effect if, as some in Paris think is all too possible, a crisis resulting from a catastrophic intensification of France's monetary and economic difficulties sweeps the General from office (as they did in April— *J.O.*). Nixon's homage to De Gaulle and his declaration of confidence in the capacities and intentions of his other hosts may be dismissed as a gamble on the healing power of flattery in Paris and as customary courtesy elsewhere. The point made here is that beneath the modest claims advanced for the European trip, before and during it and by Nixon after he returned, there was a conviction that his advent to the Presidency had presaged and already was leading to fundamental changes for the better, both in the techniques of American foreign policy and in the European scene. This in itself was neither surprising nor disturbing. What was surprising, after the preparatory emphasis upon a low-key approach to the trip, was the euphoria with which the conviction that "a new era" has arrived with Nixon was expressed in Europe.

The related proposition that the United States may now disengage (the word was never officially used) from the European allies' differences among themselves without substantive disengagement in the usual sense of the term is attractive. It would seem to make the basic commitment to European security easier to sustain. But is it really meaningful to say with Mr. Nixon's high officials that the United States is as fervently dedicated as ever to European political and economic unity but not at all concerned with the forms of unity? That we are still for the Common Market, and for Britain's admission to it, but don't much care whether the European Economic Community survives in its present form or is replaced by something else? Nixon was told in London that the British, foreseeing their indefinite exclusion from the Common Market, refuse to equate that particular frustration with total exclusion from the continental community and propose to work their way into it through every side entry that they may pry or find open. Can we, applauding and promising to support that aim, be indifferent to the means by which it is accomplished and to the probability that it will be opposed at every turn? The Nixon line that Europe's problems of this kind are "for the Europeans" to settle among and by themselves, and that the United States need only assure them that it will impartially support each of them, regardless of their differences and of whether and how the differences are reconciled, assumes a clearer distinction than actually exists between internal and external affairs and, in the interest of immediate harmony, postpones choices that no American President can indefinitely evade.

There were two clear pluses from the trip. Nixon went to Europe so early in his Presidency partly because he knew that he was distrusted there or, at best, regarded with less than adequate trust. The testimony that he won respect in every capital he visited is convincing. He appeared to know what he was about, he proved himself to be a good listener, he put life in the tired concept and promise of genuine and timely consultation with the European allies. In one of the few policy areas where material agreement with General de Gaulle was possible, Nixon all but committed himself to an early four-power conference on the Arab-Israel conflict.

One of his high officials said in Paris that the last American doubts of the value of such a conference had been removed. Nixon drew back a bit in his televised account, indicating that it was more likely than it had been, but not yet certain that the US would soon be discussing possible solutions of the Mideastern problem with France, Britain, and the Soviet Union. And discussing, he said, a big-power guarantee of the settlement, if and when the Arabs and Israelis agree on one. Will the United States be as disinterested in the form the guaranteed settlement takes as Nixon professes to be in the form of European organization? It does not seem probable.

———

The Administration did enter into four-power talks on the Middle East and continued them after their original and soon-forgotten purpose—to please De Gaulle—became moot. The Administration's intense concern with "the form the guaranteed settlement takes" became evident in late 1969.

XXIX

Back from Midway

While Richard Nixon and President Thieu of South Vietnam conferred at the naval officers' club on Midway Island, beneath a huge painting of two gooney birds cocking their bony snoots and thrusting their white breasts at each other in their majestic preliminary to copulation, I sat on the wall of an abandoned cistern in front of the enlisted men's club and communed with a live and personable baby gooney. The swarming gooneys, among them the chick who favored me with its beady stare and an occasional snap of its fearsome beak, were excellent company for a reporter who was in the throes of trying to sort the true from the false in the official accounts of why Nixon and Thieu made their long journeys to Midway and of what they undertook to accomplish there. Improbable creatures that they are, the gooneys demonstrated that the improbable is possible. By a process of association that I know to be absurd, they made it seem not only possible but likely that Nixon and his spokesmen were telling us of the accompanying press a part of the truth and implying the whole of it in their accounts of "the Midway summit."

President Thieu said after the meeting that it had been "very

useful." The "White House sources" to whom we were exposed
at President Nixon's order, before and after the meeting, agreed
with this judgment in terms that explained to my satisfaction why
President Thieu looked a good deal less happy than he said he
was when he took a farewell salute from the American honor
guard and departed for Saigon in a chartered American airliner.
I think that he realized then, as he had appeared to suspect when
he publicly requested the meeting, that Mr. Nixon has made up
his mind to do whatever he has to do in order to extricate the
United States from the Vietnam war. Neither Thieu nor the
reporters who followed Nixon to Midway and back to Washington
were told this, of course. It is a conclusion derived from what
Nixon allowed the White House sources who spoke for him to say
about the Midway meeting. It is not the conclusion that the
President's spokesmen intended to encourage. The conclusion that
they would prefer and indorse is that there is a point beyond which
the President is not prepared to go, a price larger than the price
that he is prepared to pay, in order either to end the war by
negotiation or to bring about a total American withdrawal from
it. But, assuming as I do that the President's White House sources
gave a true (though limited) account of his purposes and hopes
on the way to and back from gooney-land, I do not see how any
conclusion other than the one that I have stated can be drawn.

A word about the aforementioned "White House sources" is
necessary. The White House requires that "they" be cited in the
plural, without a name, and without direct quotation. They per-
form only on special occasions, such as Nixon's May 14 statement
of Vietnam policy and his Midway trip, when the President is
particularly anxious that the reporting and interpretation conform
with his view of the facts. They speak with his authority and, more
to the point in foreign policy matters, with the full authority of
Henry A. Kissinger, the President's assistant for national security
affairs. It became more evident than ever during the Midway trip
that Nixon's Vietnam policy is Kissinger policy. The official roster
of the delegation with Nixon at Midway listed Kissinger ahead of
Secretary of State William P. Rogers, who was also there. When
a reporter noted the fact, made clear during the trip, that the chief
American negotiator in Paris, Henry Cabot Lodge, who was also
at Midway, did not share Kissinger's heady belief that Hanoi and

the National Liberation Front were just about ready for serious negotiations, the White House sources retorted that Kissinger's estimate was the President's estimate and that was that.

The one piece of hard news that emerged from the Midway meeting was Nixon's decision to withdraw "the division equivalent" of 25,000 American troops from Vietnam by the end of August. The cautious phrasing of the announcement, and the stipulation that further withdrawals are subject to further review of the war situation, invited a suspicion that this was a token gesture. It was more than that. We were told, and I believe, that the President ordered this first withdrawal in full awareness that a mistake in his calculation of the military realities would be irretrievable. We were not told, but what we were told suggests, that he also ordered it in awareness that it begins a process of disengagement that may be slowed but cannot be halted once it has been started. His and our White House sources never mentioned the mollifying effect that it and the qualified promise of further withdrawals are intended to have upon American opponents of the war. They preferred to emphasize, though with the greatest caution, the effect that it may have upon Hanoi. The hope is that it will persuade Hanoi that it will do better to settle the war now rather than to sustain indefinite struggle with South Vietnamese forces so strengthened that they can do their own fighting, for as long as may be necessary, without the support of American combat troops. The fear, freely acknowledged, is that it may have the opposite effect of convincing Hanoi and the National Liberation Front that they have only to hold fast until the Americans bug out for good and all. The White House sources said that Nixon was timing this and future withdrawals, and determining the proportions of combat and noncombat forces to be included in them, partly to guard against the all-too-possible conclusion, in Hanoi and at home, that he was really planning and doing his best to conceal an elegant form of bugging out.

The press had done Nixon a large favor by letting its preoccupation with the advance rumors of impending troop withdrawals obscure the political issues that were actually paramount in Saigon and at the Paris negotiations, and he took advantage of the fact by making the most of his decision to begin withdrawal. It was significant, however, that before and after the Midway conference the White House sources discussed the political issues at length and with seeming frankness. Unless we on the trip were deliberately deceived, and I don't believe we were, the following may be stated as fact.

Nixon joins Thieu in rejecting, *for the present,* any deal in Paris or Saigon that would give the National Liberation Front places in an interim coalition government or that in any other way would assure the NLF a share of power in South Vietnam by any means other than popular elections. But, as Secretary Rogers said publicly before he went to Midway and as the White House sources said with maximum emphasis, the Nixon Administration is not "wedded" to the Thieu regime in the way that Washington has been committed to incumbent Saigon regimes since the 1950's. The cumulative effect of the guidance offered along the way to and from the Pacific meeting induced an impression that the Administration may very well, at some point not now foreseen, go along with a settlement that brings the NLF into a Saigon government without elections. It was said, first off and then on the reportable record, that the Administration views with calm the possibility that portions of South Vietnam may remain after the war in the control of the NLF, much as portions of the country now are, regardless of the government nominally ruling from Saigon. Nixon is on record with a willingness to admit the NLF to any mixed or international commissions that may be agreed upon in Paris to oversee elections and the political campaigns that would precede them. Such a commission or combination of commissions could and probably would, in effect, supersede the incumbent government for purposes of controlling the political processes of South Vietnam. Once the Nixon Administration accepts, as it has, the prospect of NLF participation in the actual government of South Vietnam to this extent, its formal insistence that "the will of the people" rather than the will of the Paris negotiators determine the terms and consequences of a settlement becomes a diminishing factor in the American position.

If there is a valid reason to discount the impressions reported here, it is that they arise from statements made in the hope that they will bring Hanoi and the NLF into the serious negotiations which Nixon, led to his conclusion by Kissinger, believed in June to be near at hand. When the President said upon his return from Midway that "we have opened the door to peace" and that "now we invite the leaders of North Vietnam to walk with us through that door," he was not indulging in mere rhetoric. He was expressing a hope, a hope voiced with something close to desperation by his White House sources, that is in fact the basis of the whole American position. If the same sources are to be believed, the President realizes that a bargaining position based upon gimmickry and deliberate deception would constitute the worst of follies because Hanoi and the NLF, not to mention President Thieu in Saigon, would see it for what it was and throw it back at him with disastrous consequences for him and for his hopes of settling the war.

Critics of the Nixon posture to date, along with the many who find it hard to place anything near full confidence in Richard Nixon, are under some obligation to acknowledge the extent to which he, in the interest of drawing Hanoi and the NLF into serious discussion of a bearable settlement of the war, has exposed the folly of the American presence and commitment in South Vietnam. The premise upon which the Eisenhower, Kennedy, and Johnson Administrations based the commitment and the intervention required to fulfill it was that a communist South Vietnam would endanger the security of the United States. When Nixon says that the United States is quite prepared to accept an elected all-Communist government or one that includes Communists in Saigon, and indicates that the United States no longer undertakes to preserve a non-Communist regime simply because it is non-Communist, he abandons the premise and clears the way, if such be the eventual necessity, for leaving the two Vietnams, North and South, to their own devices and fates.

On his way to Midway and on Midway, Nixon said that he does not propose to back away from or diminish "the American role in the world." How to reconcile his broad and ringing definition of that role at the Air Force Academy in Colorado Springs with his manifest desire to get out of the Vietnam war may be difficult for some people but it clearly is not for him. If he perceives any real conflict between the two positions, he is better at deception than I have thought he was.

XXX

Vietnam: Fading Hope

Those for whom the announcement in mid-September of a second reduction of American forces in Vietnam was a joyous occasion did not include Mr. Nixon and Henry A. Kissinger, the President's chief foreign policy adviser. Kissinger is known to be in a mood of profound pessimism about the prospects of bringing the war to the kind of end that he had led Nixon to think attainable, and the President must be supposed to share his mentor's deepening doubts. The Kissinger design for drawing Hanoi into the negotiation of a settlement short of "a disguised American defeat" has not worked out in a single respect since the President presented it as his own on May 14. There is no confidence at the White House that the death of Ho Chi Minh, the continuing reduction of the American combat presence in Vietnam, or any other present or foreseeable factor will set it to working. There is, on the contrary, a growing apprehension that the course principally devised by Kissinger and taken by the President has served only to convince Ho's heirs in Hanoi that they have only to wait, and not much longer, for the victory that they already claim.

One of the bitter ironies of the dilemma in which Mr. Nixon finds himself is that this possibility was foreseen. Nobody could be more aware than Henry Kissinger of the oddity of trying to bring a determined foe to the desired terms by reducing rather than increasing military pressure. When he first detailed his "generous and reasonable peace offer" in May, the President emphatically ruled out "a one-sided withdrawal from Vietnam" and proposed mutual American and North Vietnamese withdrawal "on a mutually agreed timetable." Nevertheless, the "one-sided withdrawal" now in process was contemplated from the first and was publicly added, at Midway Island, to the Kissinger design within less than a month. It was deemed necessary in order to win from the American public the patience, the time, the support for "a program which can lead to a peace we can live with and a peace we can be proud of" for which Nixon pleaded at the end of his May pronouncement.

Behind it, however, was another calculation, a calculation basic to the plans and hopes of the Administration and one that, so far, has proved to be mistaken. This was that Hanoi would perceive in the Nixon proposals and in a gradual transfer of the combat burden from American to South Vietnamese ground forces a choice between indefinitely prolonged warfare, with no chance of winning full control of South Vietnam, and a shortened war with, at its end, a chance—perhaps a very good chance—of winning that control by political rather than military means.

How Nixon and Kissinger (who has been identified elsewhere as the "White House source" who has expounded and justified the Nixon policy to the press at critical points since it was announced) could have believed or even hoped that such a choice would draw Hanoi and the Vietcong leadership into useful negotiation is a mystery if the Administration approach to peace is viewed only in its public context. One of the Administration's difficulties is that it cannot, or anyhow feels that it cannot, set forth in public and more than imply in private the true and whole context which has been conveyed to Hanoi in many ways through many channels. The offered prospect has been no more persuasive to Hanoi in the conveyed context than the public version has been to the Administration's American critics. But the President's hopes for its success, not yet dead but surely dying, become more understandable and less absurd if the implications underlying the declared policy are taken into account.

All of the important implications are inherent in the President's May statement that "we are prepared to accept any government in South Vietnam that results from the free choice of the South Vietnamese people themselves." This and the accompanying proposals for supervised elections have been interpreted to signify nothing more than a cover for American commitment to the Thieu-Ky regime in Saigon. But Hanoi and the Vietcong's political leadership have been invited to read much more than that into the official rhetoric and to believe that a result much more attractive to them is possible, if only they will enter into serious negotiation in Paris and so collaborate with the United States in lending the appearance of "free choice" to the negotiated result. Ho when he was alive, and now his heirs, have been urged to discern and believe that the United States, among other things, no longer considers that a Communist regime or a coalition regime including Communists and dominated by them, in the end if not initially, would necessarily endanger American security. This in turn is intended to be a signal to Hanoi and the Vietcong that the premise which drew the US into the war no longer obtains and that the potential range of terms for an acceptable settlement is therefore much wider than the President finds it politic to indicate publicly. Evidence of the Administration's extreme anxiety to get the point over to Hanoi, and to condition the American public for gradual disclosure of it, was provided by Secretary of State William P. Rogers at a press conference on August 20. He said openly what had previously been said only in private White House briefings: that is, that the US is willing to let the Vietcong retain control, after a negotiated end of the war, of any areas of South Vietnam that it may then occupy.

Official discretion apart, a factor that has obscured the prospect actually held out to Hanoi is the impression that the Administration is, at Kissinger's instance, committed to a "two-track" technique of negotiation—leaving the vital political negotiations to the present and manifestly intransigent Saigon regime and confining the American delegation in Paris to military issues. Nixon in fact said in May, and Hanoi has been forcefully reminded since, that the US is prepared to negotiate both military and political issues whenever Hanoi and the Vietcong leadership are ready for substantive negotiation. Hanoi has been told, by every means short of open declaration, that it may expect far more generous terms from the US than it can expect from the Saigon government—an impression that the recent appearance of dissent between Washington and Saigon over response to Hanoi's proposal of a three-day cease-fire in honor of Ho was bound and may have been intended to strengthen.

The primary reason for the President's delay in announcing his second troop reduction, originally promised for August, and the terms in which it was finally announced and explained on Sept. 16, tend to affirm all that has been said here. Private elaboration of the Nixon peace proposals having failed to lure Hanoi to substantive negotiation, and the start of "one-sided withdrawal" having patently enhanced its conviction that the US is on the run from Vietnam, the President and his advisers concluded that it was imperative to demonstrate to Hanoi that the disengagement process is not irreversible. A brief delay was the most that seemed to be politically possible at home, all that could be risked in view of domestic disenchantment with what the President has called "this dreary, difficult war." So the second reduction was a modest one (24,000 to 35,000 below September 1 levels, depending on whether you figure from authorized or actual levels); it was stretched out to December 15; and the emphasis, at the White House briefing customary on such occasions, was less upon the figures than upon the implication that the President can in fact delay or halt the whole process if Hanoi and Vietcong action in the field and at Paris moves him to do so.

The formal announcement, with its catalog of public American proposals for "meaningful negotiations," amounted to an open and all but strident appeal to Hanoi to recognize that this Administration is prepared to be flexible and sensible—these words were reiterated orally with the greatest emphasis—if only Hanoi will indicate at Paris some willingness to negotiate and compromise. *Compromise* was another emphasized word, in terms meaning that the Nixon proposals are subject to very broad compromise. Nixon himself has said that everything is negotiable except the right of free choice in South Vietnam, and the White House source who spoke for him placed no more stress than he obviously had to upon the caveat.

Questions remain, questions that will plague the Administration and compound the gloom at the White House if Hanoi continues to refuse all productive response. Why not, for a starter, acknowledge that we do not have and never had any business in Vietnam and get out? Nixon in his May speech gave the Administration's best answer to that one: ". . . The urgent question today is what to do now that we are there, not whether we should have entered on this course, but what is required of us today." If a coalition that includes Vietnamese Communists may be acceptable at some point, why not meet Hanoi's most insistent demand now and grant it now, inevitably dumping the Thieu-Ky regime when we do it? Nixon again: "That would mean a surrender on our part, a defeat on our part," and it would subject countless Vietnamese to reprisals "that would shock and dismay everyone in the world who values human life."

And—what kind of presence does the US intend to sustain in the postwar Vietnam it wants, or in a South Vietnam doing more and more of its own fighting? Nixon has said that, given real negotiation, the US would accept "a neutralist" South Vietnam, but he has yet to say just what he means by that. He also has never said, but it is quite clear, that the protracted warfare threatened as an alternative to a war ended by negotiation would require a massive, indefinite American military presence in the forms of air and naval support and perhaps 250,000 American troops—five times the number now maintained in South Korea—instructing, supplying, and otherwise assisting the "Vietnamized" Army of South Vietnam. This last, of course, is intended to repel, not attract, Hanoi and the Vietcong, but it does attract them in a curious way. They clearly assume, and the Administration fears that they rightly assume, that the American public and Congress would not tolerate that situation for very long.

A final question, the question that haunts the Nixon White House more than any other, is: what do we do if every Nixon bid for "a peace we can live with" fails as the bids to date have failed? I doubt that the President, or Henry Kissinger, or anyone else in the Administration knows the answer to that one.

———

Administration officials, principally Defense Secretary Laird, began saying in late 1969 that, failing a negotiated settlement, the "transitional" American military presence in South Vietnam might be reduced eventually to around 40,000 troops in a "training mission."

XXXI

Death to Gooks

It was in character for Mr. Nixon to handle the My Lai massacre very coolly, and he did. He arranged matters so that he didn't have to say a word about it before the press conference that he scheduled for December 8 and yet got credit 12 days earlier for the sentiment that it was "abhorrent to the conscience of all the American people." That statement was made to White House reporters on the day before Thanksgiving by the President's press secretary, Ronald Ziegler, who preceded it by saying, "I would like to give you my comment" emphasizing *my*. The most that Ziegler would add, after prolonged badgering for some indication "of how the President personally feels," was that what he had said "conveys the overall feeling of the White House and the Administration and, therefore, the President." This was accompanied by a pointed reminder that the episode "alleged in this case" occurred in March of 1968, meaning that it was the Johnson Administration's massacre, not Mr. Nixon's. We also were told that Secretary of Defense Melvin Laird first heard about it in early April of this year and reported it to the President some while after that, at a time not specified except that it was before the press and television

Osborn.

We of course frown on
this sort of Killing!

got onto it. Since he learned of it, "the President has, of course, been informed and kept informed of this matter."

Laird and Army Secretary Stanley Resor said during the period of initial furor that the allegations and the supporting evidence "shocked and sickened" them. When asked if it was true that "a dirty, jungle war" like the one in Vietnam "brutalizes large numbers of young Americans," Secretary of State William P. Rogers said on the National Educational Television network that "I don't think there is any way to deny that." Laird and Rogers expressed similar sentiments to the President and he presumably shared the sentiments. But the main and natural preoccupation at the White House was with the effect that the My Lai affair and the further disclosures, already beginning, of other casual killings of Vietnamese civilians by American soldiers would have on what Laird called "the President's program" for disengagement from Vietnam. Without "trying to make the case" that the My Lai story would "increase" public support for the President's policy, Laird said he didn't think it would "hurt." The President's staff adviser, Henry Kissinger, estimated the probable effect in about the same way. If it be true, as I was led at the White House to believe, that Mr. Nixon is in fact and in the last extreme prepared to pay any political and military price necessary to get the United States out of the Vietnam war, the judgment could be that My Lai and events like it in kind if not in degree will assist that endeavor, to the extent that they stimulate popular revulsion against the war.

The President and his advisers may be forgiven if they calculate that the revulsion will not be as great as people with tender sensibilities assume. Six days after the White House spokesman refused any direct expression of how the President "personally feels," the press had yet to record a single statement of unease or regret from nationally known churchmen. The *Wall Street Journal* reported that a large proportion of some 200 Americans questioned around the country either refused to believe the My Lai story or dismissed it with such remarks as "That's the way war is." They are among the Americans, in their uncountable numbers, who would not be displeased by Melvin Laird's reply to a question put to him by the chairman of a House subcommittee in October. Laird was asked whether renewed escalation of the war was possible if the dual Nixon effort to negotiate a settlement of the war or to pass the combat burden to the South Vietnamese failed. Laird replied that "I would not rule out that possibility completely." Mr. Nixon started saying in private, last summer, that he had ruled it out, and suggestions to the contrary are dangled more for effect upon Hanoi than to indicate at home that it is a real and remaining possibility. But a side effect of the public reaction to My Lai, if it is in the main a negative nonreaction, could be to rule the possibility in again. A public that condones or, at the least, accepts as a natural and inevitable aspect of the Vietnam war the deliberate killing of women and children by American individuals, aiming rifles and machine guns at the victims before them, might be expected to support and even welcome one more effort to win the military victory that the President foreswore last May.

The hell and the peril of it are that the deliberate killing of civilians, women and children among them, *is* a natural and inevitable aspect of the Vietnam war. It is in part and truly "a people's war," a war in which women, young girls, and young boys fight for the Vietcong and have killed and will continue to kill American soldiers. In the March 2, 1968 issue of *The New Republic,* Orville Schell told of the satisfaction that American air crews took in searching out and gunning down any and all South Vietnamese that they spotted below them in areas deemed to be hostile. Like examples, most of them unreported but many of them sure to be reported from now on, must have numbered in the thousands since—to put no earlier date on it—Americans went into ground and close air combat in Asia in 1950, in Korea. It was then (excluding World War II) that the fact that Americans should never be required to fight among or for or against people whom they call "gooks" began to be documented in blood. The Koreans were gooks, the South Vietnamese are gooks, and that is all that really needs to be said to explain My Lai. It needed especially to be said to President Nixon, who must have heard the term but who, from his experience as a privileged traveller in Asia, could not possibly comprehend all that it signifies. It signifies that the American fighting men who use the term regard the people to whom they apply it as less than human—even though, as Nixon spokesmen say, most of the Americans who say gook and think gook never knowingly shoot the gooks just because they are gooks. The problem is not racial, but national. Black Americans have said that they participated in the slaughter, comrades in horror with their white fellows.

Here I testify from knowledge of myself. On an April afternoon in 1966, I visited a hamlet in the region of My Lai with an American officer. While he was at his business, arranging to have a Vietnamese child with a harelip admitted for surgery to an American military hospital, I noticed, across the paddies, a bow-legged and very small Vietnamese man running fast—to where and for what reason, I could not know but thought then that I knew. I assumed that he was running to tell the Vietcong of our presence and I thought to myself that somebody ought to shoot the god-damned gook.

XXXII

Doubts About Vietnamization

With ever more urgency and ever less hope, the Administration has tried to get across to Hanoi the message that it will pay—it will *really* pay—to negotiate a settlement of the Vietnam war. The President brought himself to say at his press conference on December 8 that if Hanoi continues to refuse to respond to the message from Washington, it will in a distant future find the Saigon government a harder bargainer that it would find the United States now. His Secretaries of State and Defense and, behind a cloak of anonymity imposed by the White House, his staff adviser on foreign affairs, Henry A. Kissinger, strive in every way they can think of to put across the same message. They know from what they call the "feed-backs" that they get through various diplomatic channels, including Moscow, that the Hanoi Government has heard the message. What they do not know is whether the men of Hanoi have understood the message and the implication, buried in it, of readiness upon the part of this Administration to offer substantially more in the way of political concession for a viable settlement of the war than the President deems it feasible to tell either the "silent majority" that he has rallied, at least for the moment, to his support at home, or the Thieu-Ky government in Saigon.

The Nixon call to Hanoi has taken odd forms, in language that can be and is read by some people to mean that the Administration is less willing now than it was a few months ago to pay anything near the political price that will have to be paid for a negotiated settlement. The same language may also be read to mean that Mr. Nixon has let himself be persuaded that the support he has mustered for his "plan for peace" can be transformed into support for a war protracted into 1972, and perhaps even beyond, on a diminishing scale. I don't read it that way, and I hear on Capitol Hill that such Republican Senators as the veteran George Aiken of Vermont and freshmen Marlow Cook of Kentucky and Charles Mathias of Maryland don't read it that way, either. Mr. Nixon has convinced them and others, in private discussions dating from last summer, that he is determined—"come hell or high water," *Time* quotes a Senator quoting the President—to extricate the United States from this war. What I continue to hear at the White House, at a distance well removed from Mr. Nixon, suggests that he has not fully indicated, even to Senators in his confidence, the extent of the political concessions that he is prepared to offer if only Hanoi will enter at Paris into negotiations that can be made to appear to preserve for the people of South Vietnam the promised right "to determine their own fate."

If this analysis is correct, the hard language that Mr. Nixon and some of his spokesmen have adopted lately is aimed more at convincing Hanoi that it will indeed profit from early negotiation than at signalling an impending change of American tactics and purpose. Mr. Nixon's statement, in his announcement of his third troop withdrawal on December 15, that Hanoi "will find us flexible and forthcoming" when and if it agrees to "talk seriously" in Paris, was made with less emphasis than a spokesman placed upon the same assertion in September. But it was still there and it was intended to be the central message to Hanoi. The President quoted with ap-

proval a passage from a recent report to him by Sir Robert
Thompson, a British authority on anti-guerrilla warfare and a
famous advocate of sustained anti-Communist commitment in
Southeast Asia, suggesting that the right and attainable goal is to
maintain "an independent, non-Communist South Vietnam." That,
on Nixon's past record, is certainly the goal that he prefers. But,
in declaring since May that the US is prepared to accept any government chosen by fair election in South Vietnam, and by guaranteeing in advance to the Communists of Hanoi and the NLF the
right to participate in and help to supervise a negotiated election
"as an organized political force," he has renounced it as a goal
essential to American security. If "an independent, non-Communist
South Vietnam" is no longer considered vital for security reasons,
it can hardly be vital to Mr. Nixon's "plan for peace" insofar as
that plan envisages and the President prefers a negotiated settlement.

Mr. Nixon and his associates have been doing their best to
appear comfortable with the alternative that they have devised
for themselves and for South Vietnam. This is "Vietnamization,"
meaning the gradual withdrawal of American ground forces and the
transfer of combat responsibilities to the South Vietnamese Army.
It is not a very convincing best. The Administration's assertions of
confidence that the alternative is working and will continue to work
have a hollow ring when the more extreme expressions are ex-
amined closely. Secretary of Defense Melvin Laird, who is billing
himself as the inventor and chief advocate of Vietnamization, went
beyond the bounds of credibility when he assured a House subcommittee in October that Vietnamization, "in itself could lead the way
to a military victory in the sense of the South Vietnamese being
able to defend their country, even against North Vietnam." Congressman John Rhodes of Arizona said to Laird, ". . . you are
not ruling out the possibility, then, that the South Vietnamese,
when Vietnamization is completed, could actually do what is
necessary to end the war by military victory over North Vietnam?"
Laird answered, "I am not," and if his answer had stopped there
it would have been the ultimate evidence that the Administration
has been deluding itself. The full answer gave away the true, the
desperately urgent game that the President and his principal
spokesmen are playing in their effort to communicate their real

message to Hanoi. "I am not," Laird said, "and that is one of the points I would like to communicate as well as we can to Hanoi and to the other side in Paris."

In testimony before the House subcommittee and later before the Senate Foreign Relations Committee, Laird refused so much as to discuss the possibility that Vietnamization might fail. But that possibility is discussed at the White House, in an interesting way. At one of the recent background briefings through which the Nixon people sought maximum publicity for their measure of achievement in the first Nixon year, the adviser explaining Vietnam policy for the President acknowledged that the "Vietnamized" army of South Vietnam has yet to be put to a convincing test of its ability, present and potential, to assume the combat responsibilities now borne by American ground troops. He reminded his audience that the President had postponed the actual withdrawal of a third increment of troops (50,000) until after the Tet holiday season has passed in February. If the North Vietnamese and Vietcong forces try a Tet offensive in 1970, as they did in 1968 and 1969, the President's spokesman said, we may at last get a needed test of the South Vietnamese army's capabilities. It was a casual remark, hardly noted by the reporters who heard it. I thought it worthy of note, indicative of a degree of doubt and uneasiness about Vietnamization that is seldom allowed to surface. It could be interpreted as one of many indications that the Nixon Administration understands very well that the viable way out of this war is through negotiation. Whether Mr. Nixon is prepared, after nearly a year in office, to pay the price that he probably will have to pay for productive negotiation is debatable. But he, most assuredly, is prepared to pay *a* price. His diminished but abiding hope is that Hanoi will in time get and respond to the message that he is.

Secretary of State William P. Rogers has said that any time Hanoi's representatives in Paris feel that the Americans are misreading the other side's intentions, "all they have to do is pick up the phone and tell us." Could it be that all that Mr. Nixon has to do is "pick up the phone"? I get an impression at the White House, notwithstanding the current claim that there have been "11 private talks" without result, that the President and Secretary Rogers and Henry Kissinger are reluctant to communicate their message in so simple a way. It just might be worth a try.

———

The Tet season of 1970 passed without an enemy offensive and the test that it would have provided.

XXXIII

Changed Feeling

I have been trying to formulate intelligibly, for myself and others, what I know and feel about Mr. Nixon that I didn't know and feel at the moment on January 20, 1969 when he took his oath. It is not an easy task, and I find upon inquiry among other reporters who have watched him from the dubious vantage of the West Wing lobby at the White House that they share my difficulty. Ask them to set aside the public record of his formal actions in the Presidency and tell you what they know now that they didn't know then about the man in the Presidency, and they typically reply, "Why, nothing—not a damn thing, now that I think about it."

I know, from observation rather than hearsay, exactly one personal thing about Mr. Nixon that I didn't know after following him around the country in his 1968 campaign. He dyes his hair. He does it in order to conceal the spreading grey at the forward fringes, in his modest sideburns. This I discovered on the hot September night when he paused at Gulfport, on his way back to Washington from his autumn month in California, and was all but mobbed by thousands of white Mississippians who had assembled at the airport, amid the ruins left by hurricane Camille, to demonstrate their gratitude for what they understood to be his sympathetic view of their racial problems and attitudes. When he broke out of the adoring mob and climbed the steps of Air Force I, his dark hair was wet with sweat. The dye had washed away, revealing the

grey in his sideburns. I had never seen it before and I have not seen it since. Nor have I heard it mentioned by the assistants who habitually plead, when pressed for detail about the President as a person, that "Mr. Nixon is a very private man."

Two events during his stay in San Clemente at the end of his first year in office suggested that this very private President was trying, at the start of his second year, to correct the impression that he is so closely guarded, by himself and by his staff, because he is afraid to show himself in ways and situations that may expose to general view the man within the shell. On New Year's morning, at the signing of a bill requiring him to substitute a statutory environmental council for the one he had created on his own authority, he appeared to the reporters whom he joshed and allowed to josh him, just a little, to be wholly at ease, really enjoying the occasion and the exposure that went with it. On the first Saturday afternoon of 1970, he let TV cameras record and scores of newsmen observe his dubbed drive and his mediocre second drive from fhe take-off tee at a Los Angeles country club. One of his assistants, watching the President hunched over the ball, the image of a duffer soon to be seen on the tube by millions of other duffers, wailed that the staff would never have let it happen if they had realized how cruelly and thoroughly exposed he would be at that instant. Mr. Nixon seemed to one of the watchers, Robert Semple of *The New York Times,* to be in a state of "controlled agony," doing for effect the sort of thing that does not come naturally for him.

The differences that a year of observation made in my feeling about Nixon the President are easier to summarize than the little that I have learned about the man. In 40 years of reporting, no public figure repelled me as Nixon the candidate did in 1968. With his simplistic distortions, his shoddy appeal to the Wallace vote in the South and nationally, the packaged crowds and the synthetic situations that the candidate's advance men contrived for him, Mr. Nixon seemed to me to go far beyond the bounds of deception allowed to politicians in our system. Tactics apart, the viewed Nixon—the sullen mouth twitching on order into that spurious smile, the quality of cold and unceasing calculation to be seen in his little eyes—aroused in me a sense of ingrained and ineradicable cheapness. It was incredible to me, all the polls and other indicators notwithstanding, that this man could be the President of the United States.

It still is, to a degree. I understood the reporter who stood beside me in the White House rose garden, watching Mr. Nixon with a visitor on the portico outside his Oval Office, and murmured to himself, "I still can't believe it, I just can't believe it." But that feeling of incredulity passes with time, and now, for me, it is all but gone. There Mr. Nixon is, in the Presidency, changing with it and growing in it in ways dimly and uncertainly perceived, but somehow attractive in a sense that nothing about him attracted me in 1968.

In part, of course, it is a matter of fascination with the office and with the effect that its power and majesty must have upon the least majestic of the men who attain it. I have a feeling that the Presidency has been good for Richard Nixon, in a distinctly therapeutic way. Probably without realizing all that they were implying, some of his closest associates in the campaign made his need for the kind of therapy that I have in mind very clear with their stories of the elaborate care taken to preserve his energies, to protect him from unexpected confrontations and crises, and—above all—to save him when they could from a renewal of the deep hurts that the press and two public rejections, for the Presidency in 1960 and for the governorship of California in 1962, had caused him. The Nixon who clawed his way to the peak in 1968 was, if such stories were true, a profoundly injured and fearful man, inwardly uncertain of his capacity to withstand another climactic defeat and uncertain, too, of his capacity to deal with sudden troubles for which he had not prepared himself or been prepared by others. He still needs the protective preparation. With the continuing expansion and reorganization of his staff structure, he has gone to extraordinary lengths to make sure that he gets it. But, given it and the confidence that must have come to him with his attainment of the office so long sought and so long denied him, Nixon the President seems to me to have become a stronger man, a more decent and credible man, than Nixon the congressman, the senator, the Vice President, and the candidate allowed himself to be. It is as if the Presidency enabled and encouraged him to afford a showing of strength, a level of decency that his character did not require and his circumstances did not permit in the prior time.

I am not as sure that Nixon in the Presidency will be good for the country in the succeeding years as I am that his first year in the office was good for him. Yet it is reasonable to hold that what is good for a President, in the meaning of the term that I have tried to convey here, is likely to be of some good to the country and may be of great good.

A President who suffered from and failed to rise above the weaknesses that candidate Nixon seemed to me to suffer from would have been a disaster for the country, and this President has not been that. After the Johnson years, we know how much the country needs a credible President, and to the extent that Mr. Nixon has given us one he has served us well. With his declared and, I believe, genuine intent to disengage from the Vietnam war, and with proposals that constitute an enormous advance toward a humane and sensible national welfare system, he has recognized and moved to meet at least some of the country's larger needs. I value and quite possibly overvalue these aspects of the first Nixon year because they indicate to me a capacity, limited though the demonstration has been and flawed though it has been by the less attractive aspects that Vice President Agnew and Attorney General Mitchell express and personify, to be a better President than I thought the candidate of 1968 capable of being. If so lame and grudging an apology for Richard Nixon makes me a candidate for membership in his silent majority, so be it. I suspect that his majority includes a great many Americans who expected little that was good from him and are therefore pleased with the little more that he gave us in his first year.

———

After my report that Mr. Nixon "dyes his hair" appeared, White House assistants who see the President every day convinced me that he has convinced them and his barber that he doesn't. They failed to convince me that he does nothing whatever to conceal the grey in his mop. He does conceal it, or did until it was reported that he does.